CREATIVE STITCHERY

CREATIVE STITCHERY

Dona Z. Meilach

Lee Erlin Snow

HENRY REGNERY COMPANY
CHICAGO

For Mel Meilach
 Herb and Dana Snow

All photos by Dona Z. Meilach unless otherwise credited.

Library of Congress Catalog No. 76–126158
Published by Henry Regnery Company,
114 West Illinois Street, Chicago, Illinois 60610

Contents

Foreword

Creative Stitchery emphasizes needlework as a medium for the creative artist. Stitchery has become more than embroidery; it has developed as an art form, with all the potential for expressive, artistic exploration and growth. Examples illustrate the directions and growth of stitchery as it is practiced by artists and craftsmen with imagination and creativity.

The ideas and methods presented are offered to stimulate everyone interested in art to pick up needle, thread, and fabrics and to explore his potentials. Stitchery is for the man or woman willing to experiment with inexpensive, easily accessible materials; for the art teacher seeking new approaches for teaching design, color, texture, pattern, form, and all aspects of artistic endeavor. It is an invaluable source of satisfaction for professionals and amateurs, for all ages and both sexes. Creative stitchery is a medium as much for men as for women.

We wish to thank the artists, galleries, museums, teachers, students, and collectors who have cooperated in gathering materials for this book. All credits accompany the photographs. In addition, special thanks are due to Linda Caldwell, Museum of Contemporary Crafts, New York, and to Dorothy Garwood of The Egg and the Eye Gallery, Los Angeles, for their suggestions; and to Ben Lavitt and Harold Smolen (Astra Photo Service, Chicago) and Steve Kilgore (California Camera, Los Angeles) for their help in achieving the high quality of photographic prints.

Dona Z. Meilach
Lee Erlin Snow

CREATIVE STITCHERY

ORGANIC GROWTH. Esther Feldman. 4′ high, 3′ wide. Fabrics, threads, leather, buttons, beads, and knitting applied to a burlap base explode in a burst of color and activity. Such expressiveness is akin to contemporary movements in painting, though one achieves a completely different effect of texture and pattern with fabrics than with painting.

1 What's Contemporary About Stitchery?

Creating designs with needle and thread is almost as old as mankind. Like all other crafts, stitchery had its origin in the daily needs of humanity. Early examples of Oriental embroideries show that once the problem of joining two pieces of material arose, the seam was created, and it was treated decoratively. Whether the first needle was a sharp fish bone, a thorn, or a pointed stick, there appeared an instinct to surpass the limits of mere utility and to indulge in decoration.

Stitchery, or embroidery, as it was generally termed for centuries, may be defined as surface decoration applied with a needle to woven fabric. Contemporary stitchery still conforms to that definition, but the designs and methods of decorating the base fabric are so different from what was done before that, in the future history of textiles, twentieth century stitchery could well become a chapter in itself.

Stitchery has burst beyond the limits of a decorative craft. It has become an expressive art form; many fine examples hang in serious art collections along with expressionist, pop, op, and other avant-garde concepts of two- and three-dimensional art. No longer is stitchery relegated to "busy work" for proper ladies. Men, women, art students, artists, and craftsmen are adding needle and thread to their art materials as they recognize the untapped potentials of the medium.

Contemporary stitchery tends to exploit the inherent textures of fabrics and their combinations. It reflects the thinking and visual perceptions of its sister art forms such as painting, sculpture, ceramics. Contemporary stitchery may hang on a wall or sit on a pedestal as readily as does a painting or sculpture. The idea of flat surfaces is popular; in addition, there are forms that project from surfaces, hang beyond the frame, and often utilize space itself as a vital part of the composition.

Contemporary stitchery methods employ established techniques but explore new avenues. The innovative use of traditional stitches by today's stitchers has resulted in experimentation with abstract, yet artistically disciplined, statements. Ultimately, stitches are as secondary to design and interpretation as the type of paint is to a painting. Therefore, to emphasize the nature of contemporary design, the variety of stitches presented is minimal. Artists interviewed consistently reveal that modern stitchery is more dependent upon concept than upon technique. Purism and tradition in stitches and methods are passé. Today, any stitch is acceptable, any material, any combination. Most important is the aesthetically pleasing result—the form and cohesion that will satisfy the vision of the creator.

To appreciate the direction contemporary stitchery has taken, it is helpful to review the tradition from which it departs.

Very few textiles have survived from before the beginning of the Christian era, but sculptural and painted representations of garments from Babylonia, Assyria, and Egypt clearly show that surface decorations were applied to fabrics. Earliest European embroideries survive from graves in Cri-

4

Embroidered Skirt Detail. Isle of Crete. 18th century. Flowers, animals, and repeat motifs carefully embroidered in tightly controlled patterns. COURTESY, ART INSTITUTE OF CHICAGO

mea and Turkestan. Designs in wall hangings were flat embroideries depicting scenes of horses with riders and many motifs associated with Greco-Roman art from about 500 B.C. to the first century A.D.

Embroidered fabrics from an even earlier millennium probably existed in India among the highly cultured early civilizations. In India embroidery is still flourishing today as a folk art.

Throughout western history, surviving embroidered fabrics after the birth of Christianity were used for ecclesiastical decoration: for mantles, tapestries, and clothing that combined embroidery and weaving. Subjects often were scenes from the New Testament, such as the Annunciation, Last Supper, or the Resurrection. A strong Byzantine influence existed for

hundreds of years showing frontal design and predominantly gold coloration.

The best-known secular work dates from the late eleventh century. This is the famous 231-foot-long Bayeux Tapestry, actually created of wool stitched to a linen backing. The entire subject shows a vigorous and dramatic account of events that led up to the Norman conquest of England. Other secular uses for embroidery included intricately decorated tunics of noblemen and the dress of royalty and its entourage.

Domestic embroidery flourished during the Italian Renaissance. Linen embroideries used in the household were an innovation, and by the sixteenth century published pattern books were popular. Designs emulated illustrated manuscripts

CHASUBLE. Henri Matisse. 1950. Violet silk with green and blue applique. Matisse's motifs, familiar from his paintings and paper collages, also appeared in his stitchery work. COLLECTION: THE MUSEUM OF MODERN ART, NEW YORK. GIFT OF MRS. GERTRUDE A. MELLON

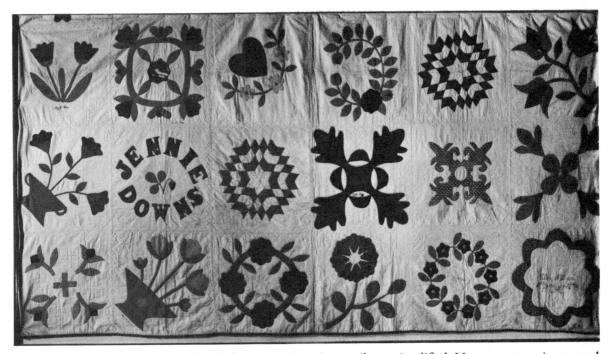

The floral designs appliqued on this 19th-century American quilt are simplified. No one pattern is repeated in exactly the same color or pattern combination. COURTESY, ART INSTITUTE OF CHICAGO

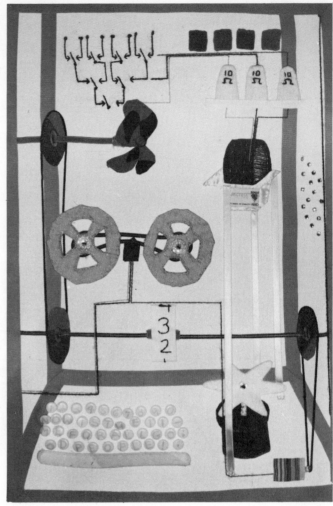

RENDER TO CAESAR. Norman Laliberte. A contemporary liturgical stitchery. COURTESY, THE UNIVERSITY OF CHICAGO

THE COMPUTOR. Harlene Schwartz. 25″ high, 20″ wide. Contemporary influences inspire the modern stitcher. PHOTO, BRENT LOWENSOHN

with ornate borders and repeat motifs. They were used for household hangings, valances, carpets, cushions, and pillow covers, along with clothing such as hats, jackets, skirts, tunics, and vests.

In the seventeenth century floral ornamentation blossomed in the ornate style characteristic of the taste of the time. Biblical scenes and classical legends were popular. Canvas and crewel work, termed "needlework" and held to be different from surface embroidery, became a widespread pastime for gentle ladies.

By the 1850s Swiss manufacturers, using an embroidery-making machine developed in 1829, caused a marked decline in hand embroidery, though fine examples on clothing and linen were still being produced in other countries. Early American settlers made embroidered household articles. All kinds of needlework flourished, utilizing traditional floral, animal, and other well-worked designs.

Efforts to introduce modern designs and to revive hand embroidery in England were made by William Morris and his followers at the turn of the twentieth century. This activity created a revival of interest in fabric decoration but not in contemporary design. Though art-nouveau

FROM LITTLE ACORNS. Dagmar Dern. 17″ high, 11″ wide. Soft hanging mounted on barrel staves. Yarns of wool, viscose, raffia, and silk suggest textural quality of bark on a background of raw silk. PHOTO, LEONORA HART

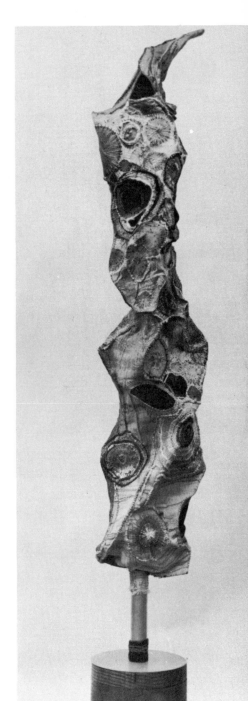

and Bauhaus influence prospered in other art forms, flowers, animals, and traditional designs continued to be used in embroidery, and those who embroidered were oblivious to modern artistic interpretation.

This book introduces a new approach to stitchery design, form, and methods that is uniquely late-twentieth century. The artists responsible have been generous in sharing their perceptions and methods. The examples are offered not to be copied but to motivate the reader to approach his own work with freedom, experimentation, and originality; to express his individual ideas through the colors and textures of fabrics and yarns.

APPLE TREE. Anna M. Sunnergren. 7′ high. Burlap, wool, and velvet over a pole and wire armature creates a "sculptural stitchery." PHOTO, ARTIST

2   Let's Begin

To do stitchery, one needs, mainly, the interest. Materials are minimal and easily accessible. Stitches can be as simple as pushing a needle in and out of a fabric or as complicated as one wishes. Knowing many stitches and involved ways of using them does not guarantee beautiful, creative work. The trick is what you do with the stitches. If stitchery instructions showing scores of stitches with strange sounding names dismay you, be assured that almost all stitches are simply variations of the few basic stitches. Often the same stitches have two or three names, which only adds to the confusion.

Many of the examples in this book have been accomplished with two or three simple-to-do stitches, using a variety of materials and yarns. Other examples combine all ten of the stitches demonstrated with some variations. But it must be emphasized that it isn't how many stitches you know that leads to creative results, it's how you take advantage of those stitches to make your designs.

There is no one best way to work. Each stitcher develops methods best suited to himself. You should do the same. Materials and methods are suggested to give you a start, to help you overcome any apprehensions you may have about how and where to begin. Once you begin, let the stitches fall where they may as you are caught up in the fascination of stitchery as an art form.

Materials

Because stitchery involves decorating a base fabric with other materials, you will need, primarily, a material on which to work. This is a matter of "anything goes." With trial and error, you'll discover that you prefer certain materials for your individual purposes. It is advisable to learn the stitches first on a piece of fabric that will be referred to as a "sampler," an "exercise material" on which to practice your stitches, see how they work, what they do, how they combine with other stitches, how they differ as you use different yarns and threads, and how they appear when you use other materials with them.

For the sampler, use heavy cotton, homespun, wool, or a linen type material that is loosely woven and sturdy. The sampler might be a left-over from a sewing project, a part of an old wool coat or skirt, or a remnant purchased at your fabric store.

If you begin with your sampler no smaller than one yard square, you'll develop a tendency to stitch more freely and in larger, bolder designs than if you work on a smaller piece of material. But use anything available. You can always change to a larger piece. A solid color is preferable to a print so that you will be able to see the effect of the stitches more readily.

The type or size of needle will vary with the fabric: large needles for heavier yarns and thick materials; smaller needles for finer threads and fabric. Look for embroi-

Materials for stitchery: Loosely woven fabrics for backgrounds; assorted yarns and threads including metallic sewing thread, rayon, perle cotton, embroidery floss, linen, thick and thin knitting yarns, of any and every color, texture, variety; wide-eyed needles, pins, scissors, feathers, beads, and assorted items to be stitched to the backing. Thimble and tailor's chalk are handy.

dery needles, tapestry needles, self-threading needles, etc., that are made with large eyes. Small-eyed needles slow down your work as you struggle to thread them. They may also prevent you from experimenting with thicker threads. Needle threaders are available and easy to use. Needles may be kept in a used pill bottle or other small container. You will also need pins and scissors.

For stitchery, you need varieties of threads and yarns. Anything and everything may be used for surface stitching. Learn to rummage through yarn counters in needlework sections of department stores and in knitting, needlework, and weaving shops for assorted yarns and threads. The types available may astonish you. There are threads so lightweight you

can hardly hold them and yarns as thick as a sailor's rope. Wools, cottons, silks, synthetics in gloss and dull finishes are available. Now that yarn manufacturers have learned to use bright dyes, particularly in the synthetic yarns, colors are lovely and available in great variety. Yarn sources advertised in needlework magazines offer a fantastic assortment, and a postcard will bring a catalogue and samples. To the stitcher, a knowledge of yarns is as important as a knowledge of paints is to the painter. Both must know textures, colors, finishes, and how all work together.

In addition to threads and yarns, accumulate scraps of fabric from old clothes, from your friends' old clothes, from everywhere, for fascinating stitcheries with multiple fabrics. Still using basic stitches, you

PORTION OF A SAMPLER. Lucy Anderson. A yard of heavy, dark green wool served as material for this brilliantly decorated sampler. The purpose is to learn stitches and how they interrelate with one another and with appliqued fabrics. The sampler itself can become a wildly creative item. A sampler may be hand held or placed on a table or on the lap to work as opposed to working on a frame.

can also incorporate feathers, beads, shells, wood, leather, pods, etc., on stitcheries for richer surface texture. Fabrics combined to make an artistic statement result in some of the most exciting and creative contemporary stitcheries.

Many of the stitches shown may also be done as "detached" stitches, that is, stitches in which only the first and last stitches are anchored to the fabric; the others are done through a first layer of stitches. This method gives greater surface texture. It is particularly successful with the chain, buttonhole, and other looped stitches.

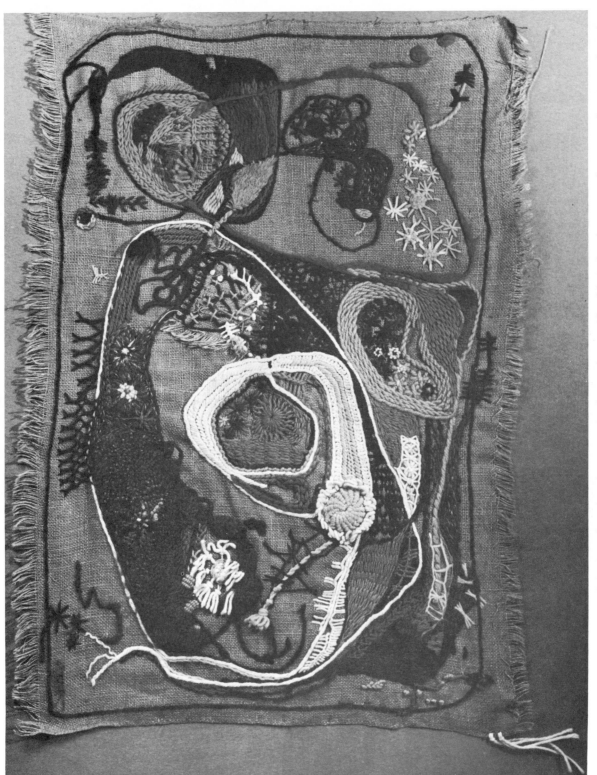

SAMPLER. Esther Feldman. 36″ high, 28″ wide. Blue-green burlap is the sampler fabric for the array of yarns and variety of stitches the artist used. Notice that stitches vary in direction, in height, some go over others, and some rughooking also is done.

SAMPLER. Esther Feldman. 32″ high, 34″ wide. A bird shape is composed of almost all the types of stitches shown on the following pages. It is surrounded by abstract combinations of stitches in a free spacing. While the sampler is not necessarily meant to be "composed" as a finished work, one should strive to work shapes of stitches in relation to one another for practice.

The Stitches

With your sampler materials in hand and your needle and thread, you are ready to learn the stitches. On unframed fabric (framing is demonstrated in Chapter 4) simply fold the fabric around the area on which you'll be working, but don't let the folded material encumber your working spot or you'll stitch several layers together.

On the following pages there are ten basic stitches plus one canvas stitch. These may be varied to result in almost as many combinations as the alphabet makes words. They are all easy to do. They are quickly perfected by men, women, and children of all ages.

It's a good idea to use a thread almost as long as your arm. If threads are too long, your arm tires and thread frazzles.

Knot your thread at one end, and push your needle through the sampler from the back, so that the knot is underneath. Follow the stitch demonstrations until you can make the movements without looking at the directions. Use different threads. Try linens, cottons, wools, orlon yarns, crewel yarns, even string (if it will go through your needle and fabric). Each yarn has individual characteristics when made into stitches and combined with other yarns. For example, you can fill in an area more quickly with thick yarns than with thin yarns, though both may be used together, depending upon the area to be filled. This is where individual choice and creativity are exercised.

Remember, the sampler is practice. It is something to work on, to use as a learning device. But it can be a project you'll be proud of. One of the beauties of stitchery is that you can't really make a mistake. If you don't like the result of one yarn on a fabric, simply take it out and try another.

Experiment with many colored yarns and fabrics also. If you are using a dark fabric for your sampler, use mostly bright-color yarns: reds, yellows, oranges, blues, greens. On a beige, white, or gray background, try earthy colors: ochers, olives, browns. You will discover that placing yarns of two hues of a color next to one another can create a completely different color to the eye. Mixing yarns is not too different from mixing paint pigments.

Some threads and fabrics are not very satisfactory; by learning to avoid these less useful varieties, you will make longer lasting and more successful stitcheries. Burlap, for instance, tends to fade after it has been exposed to the light and sun. If a burlap backing is used, plan to cover it completely. Cotton embroidery floss with six thin strands tends to separate and tangle. But a word of caution: even when you find materials or threads you prefer, always continue to experiment with more and more materials. Don't permit a set range of materials to limit your creativity. It is better to let your ideas dictate your materials than to let a narrow range of materials limit your ideas.

Use silvers, golds, and all kinds of novelty threads. If you're not sure how they'll look in a stitchery, pretest them on a sampler or pin them on your fabric. If you like the effect, use it—if not, take out the pins. All stitches and fabrics may also be combined with sewing-machine stitchery.

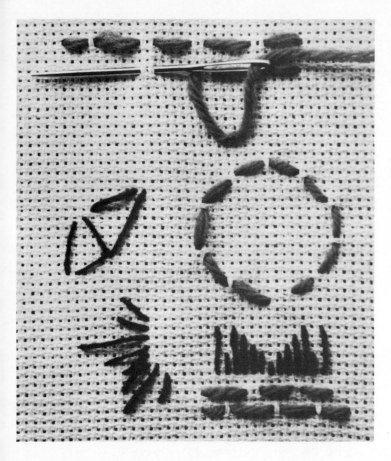

Running Stitch, or Straight Stitch

The running stitch is simple: a marvelous general purpose stitch. You simply bring the needle in and out of the fabric. You can make short stitches, long stitches, or both short and long. It can be used to outline an edge or to fill in an area. It may be run on a straight line, along a curve. You can use it to make star shapes and many unusual designs in every direction. Combine colors, thicknesses of thread, overlay one stitch on another as well as one stitch next to another.

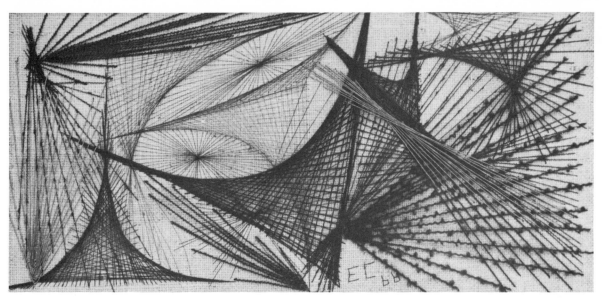

AHAZUERAS. Estelle Carlson. 12″ high, 24″ wide. Woolen and metallic threads of different color and weight in contrasting short and long variations of the running or straight stitch. COURTESY, ARTIST

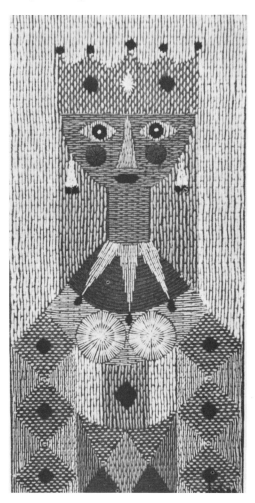

KING AND QUEEN. William Paul Baker. The running stitch in muted beiges and browns creates these geometric figures. COURTESY, ARTIST

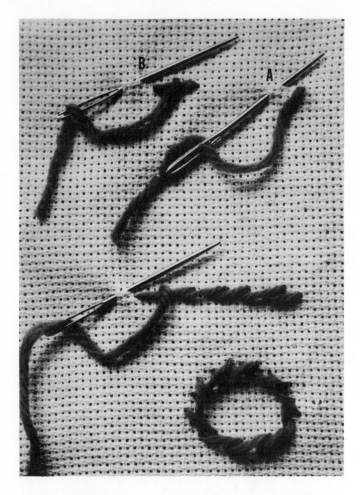

Backstitch or Stem Stitch

Begin the backstitch by bringing thread up through fabric. (A) Insert needle as though making a running stitch but bring point of needle back to middle of first stitch. Leave the loop of thread *below* needle. (B) Continue to make these stitches by bringing each new stitch only halfway to middle of previous stitch.

Backstitch may be used for outlining and as a filler. It may be made in a straight line and its length varied. It is perfect for flower stems and for borders. It may curve and it may twist.

Cross Stitch

Cross stitches may be made as individual crosses or as a row of crosses. Simply make one stitch on an angle (A) and pass another stitch across it (B). This is the same as making one running stitch over another on an angle. You can vary the size and the length of each leg of the cross for different effects. By passing a third stitch over the first two crossed stitches (C), you can make a star. You can build up a tufted star effect by making one stitch over another.

Place the "legs" of the cross stitch next to one another and you will have what many call a basket stitch. Or make the legs smaller at one end and cross them at the bottom and the result is a herringbone stitch. All may be made in straight lines, in curves, individually or in groups. Groups should go in the same direction.

MOUNT ST. VICTOIRE. Lee Erlin Snow. Cross stitches: left top and center; backstitches in varying lengths and running stitches predominate in this landscape. Observe the different directions and sizes of the stitches used to simulate the many shapes and directions of mountains. The stitches are also used to applique or attach nets and silk organzas for color shifts, shapes, and surface interest. PHOTO, DAN HELFANT

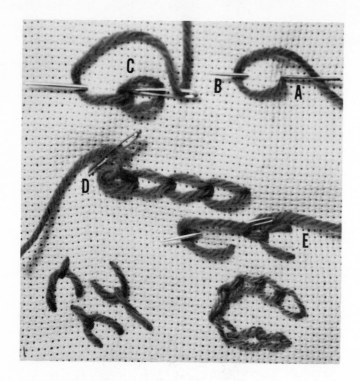

The following four stitches are made by looping the thread under the point of the needle.

Lazy Daisy and Chain Stitch

(A) Bring needle up from back of fabric. (B) Make a loop length of desired stitch, ¼″, ½″, etc., and have loop come under needle point and pull the needle through. (C) For second link, place needle in tip of first link next to upcoming thread. Repeat. (D) To end, tack at end stitch, as shown. (E) The stitch may also be made open by placing the needle above the original stitch.

Use these stitches for heavy outlines and in rows of many directions.

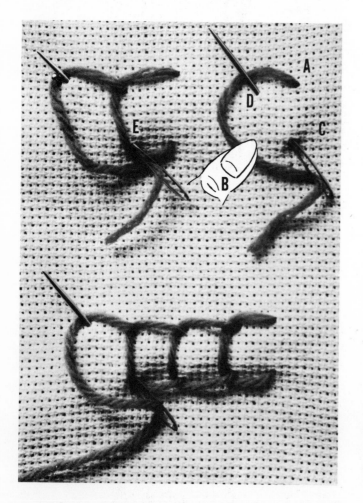

Open Ladder or Open Chain Stitch

The open ladder stitch has a looser, wider loop construction than the other stitches shown. (A) Bring thread to top of fabric. (B) Loop the thread down and around. (C) Place needle parallel with first thread but several rows below and leave the loop loose. Hold thumb at point B. (D) Place needle on angle so point of needle will be at top corner of loop. Pull needle through. (E) Insert needle at bottom corner of loop (at B, where you held the loop with your thumb) to complete first ladder rung and continue to make additional rungs.

Feather Stitch

The feather stitch is also made by placing the needle over a looped thread. (A) Begin by bringing needle up from back and making a loop. (B) Insert needle in any direction away from original stitch and (C) bring needle point through on top of loop and pull through. For second stitch (D) place needle in any direction about a 45° angle away from last stitch and make another loop (E) bringing point of needle out on top of it.

Below are directions and varieties one can achieve by stitching in different threads or curves.

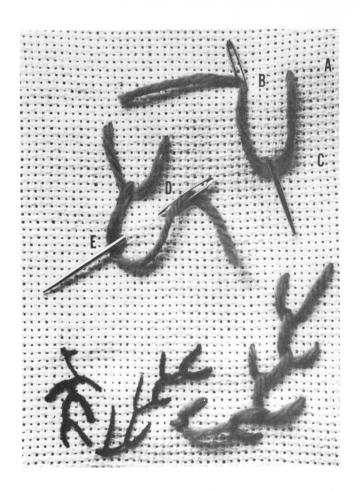

Blanket or Buttonhole Stitch

A versatile stitch, easy to make and vary. (A) Bring thread up to top of fabric and make a loop. (B) Insert needle several rows above beginning stitch. (C) Bring needle point out parallel with beginning stitch and over the thread. Pull. (D) Continue for rows of stitches.

The stitch may be varied by making the heights of the stitches differ, by changing directions of stitches, some up, some down. A thick yarn may be overlaid with a thinner yarn of the same or of a different color and texture.

When stitches are placed very close to one another, this stitch is usually called a buttonhole stitch.

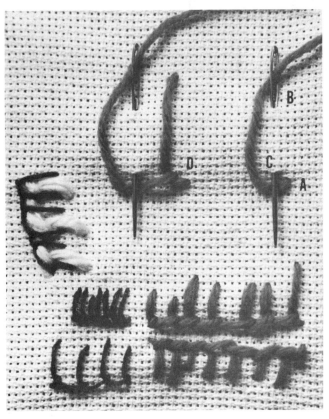

FIREBALL. Henry Stahmer. 45″ high, 40″ wide. Design suggested by bleaching background (*see* page 51) and worked completely with chain, open ladder, and blanket stitches. Study stitches carefully to observe closed and open chain stitches, the rhythm of the blanket stitches. In some areas chain stitches have been developed over the verticals of the blanket stitches.

PINK ON PINK. Lee Erlin Snow. 12″ high, 18″ wide. Chain, running, blanket, back, and cross stitches are used around edges and within composition. Background is purple Dansk linen place mat. PHOTO, DAN HELFANT

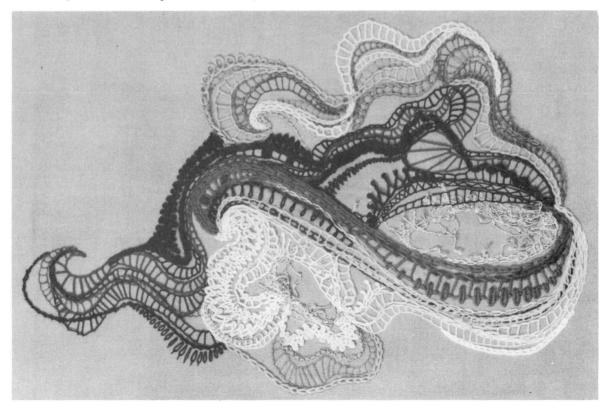

STITCHERY. Barbara Jean Adams. 22″ high, 30″ wide. Only chained stitches are used. Composition composed of a wide range of blue yarns on an avocado green cotton background. Working with one stitch to create an endless variety of forms is a stimulating and challenging design concept. COURTESY, ARTIST

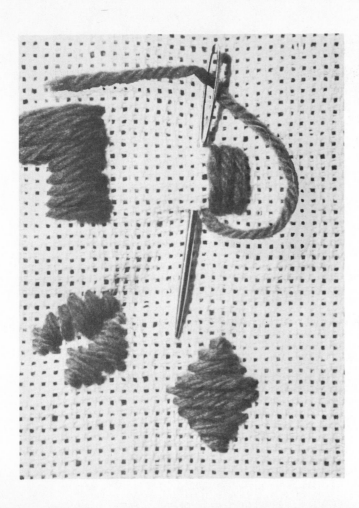

Satin Stitch

The satin stitch is a filler stitch. It is made simply by placing one straight stitch next to another straight stitch until the desired area is covered. Stitches may be used to create a filled-in area or circles. If you are working on a circle, make your first stitch the longest at the center of the circle, and gradually shorten each adjacent stitch until a circle results.

COOL CIRCLE. Pat Malarchar. 12″ square. Purple, blue, and green woolen thread worked completely in a satin stitch on linen fabric.
COURTESY, ARTIST

SAM'S THING (detail). Esther Feldman. The white free-form shapes utilize a satin stitch to hold leather remnant from the cut sole of a shoe. The satin stitch completely covers the leather shape while holding it to the upholstery background. The result, compared to other stitches, is a raised area.

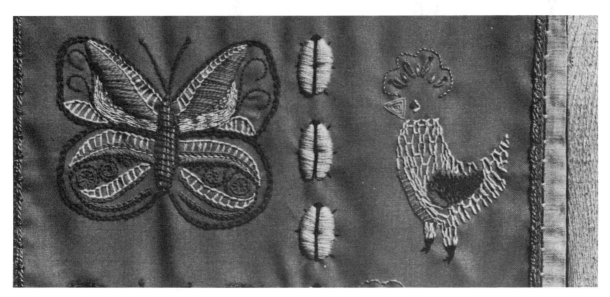

MID-SUMMER (detail). Dagmar Dern. The bodies of insects and the shapes within the butterfly wings are satin stitched. Observe the use of different shapes of chain and open ladder stitches for the butterfly wing design and for the body of the chicken. PHOTO, LEONARA HART

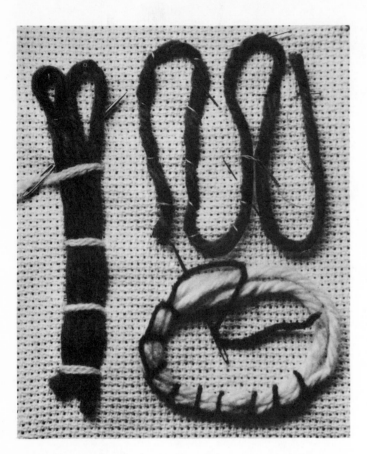

Couching

Couching is the process of attaching or holding a thread to a surface by means of another thread. Simply lay thread to be couched on fabric, pinning into place if necessary. A great variety of stitches may be used to secure thread to fabrics. Blanket, chain, and cross stitches, among others, are all excellent for this purpose. The couched yarn may consist of single or multiple rows. Placement, angle, color, size of couching threads add to the variety possible.

Couching may be considered an applique of yarn to a fabric and is usually used when a yarn is too heavy to penetrate the base fabric, or when special effects are desired.

White yarn is being couched with sewing machine thread to hold it to a felt surface and to emphasize cut-out shapes.

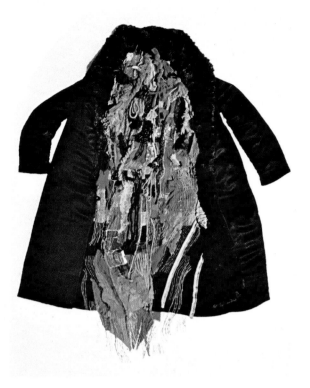

Opera Coat, Marilyn Pappas.

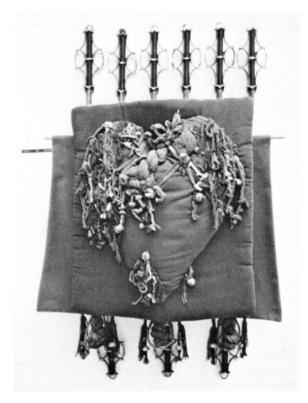

Homage to Love, Jeanne Boardman.

Jungle Fantasy, Susan H. Brown.

Lampshade for Tamis, Doris Hoover.

Opera Coat. Marilyn Pappas. 62″ high, 45″ wide. Fabric collage of fur coat with satin and yarns on a linen backing.
JOHNSON COLLECTION: "OBJECTS U.S.A."

Homage to Love. Jeanne Boardman. Stuffed velvet forms with stitchery mounted on a welded metal frame backing.
COURTESY, ARTIST

Jungle Fantasy. Susan H. Brown. 36″ high, 26″ wide. Ragged sisal sack with colored cotton linen and wool yarns tied and stitched. Macaw and blue jay feathers stitched on.
COURTESY, ARTIST

Lampshade for Tamis. Doris Hoover. 20″ high, 14″ wide, 14″ deep. Wire frame with nylon net and stitchery in wool, cotton, rayon, silk, and Swisstraw.
PHOTO, MARGARET VAILE

UNITARIAN MURAL (detail). Blanche Carstenson. A variety of threads, plain, textured, thick, and thin, is couched in single and in multiple rows. The wavy-lined threads are two layers of different threads couched to the background. COURTESY, ARTIST

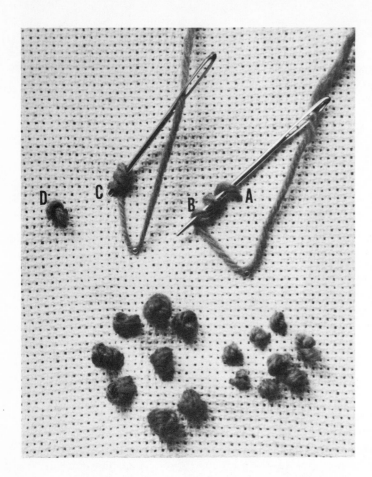

French Knot

Making the French knot seems complicated to many people, but doing it is really very simple, once you get the feel of it. The trick is how to hold the needle and your fingers to prevent the thread from slipping, and the method is shown in the accompanying photos. The principle of this is: (A) Bring thread up to top of fabric. (B) Wind needle with thread three times and then (C) Insert needle down through the fabric next to the point where thread came up. (D) Pull through. The triple wind is knotted to base.

French knots often are used in groups to create a high tactile quality—perfect for centers of flowers. They can be used anywhere the artist feels they will serve the compositional purpose. For thicker knots use thick yarn or two strands of a thread. Also vary the number of times the yarn is wound around the needle.

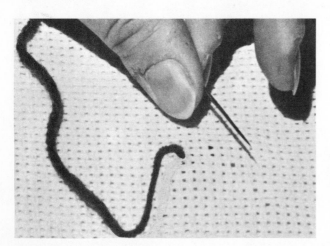

Bring threaded needle to top of fabric holding it between your thumb and third finger.

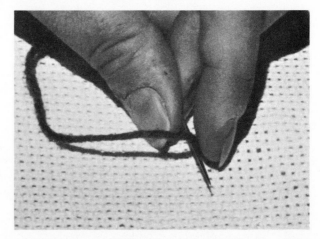

Place needle under thread, as shown, at point where thread emerges from fabric, and hold with your index finger.

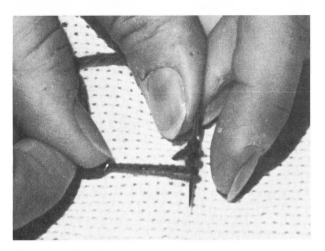

Hold needle close to fabric and make three winds with your other hand close to tip of needle.

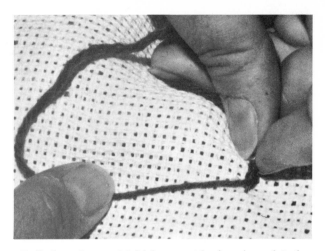

Pull thread taut. Hold loops with thumb and index finger to prevent them from slipping, and push needle down through fabric close to where thread came up, but *not* in the same hole.

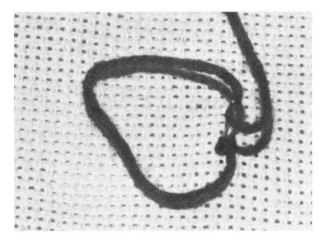

As needle is pulled through, the loose thread catches the loops and creates knot.

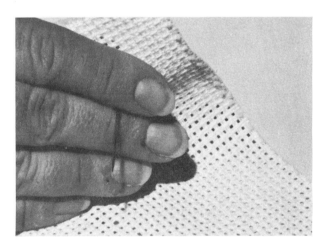

Pull needle through to bottom of fabric by holding fingers close together and flat on the fabric.

PHILIPPINE EMBROIDERY (detail). Clusters of French knots are made with raffia to simulate flower centers. Satin stitches in multi-colors fill in petal forms. COLLECTION: DONA MEILACH, CHICAGO

FLOWER. Jo Mineer. Use of small and large French knots as a filler stitch. COLLECTION: MR. AND MRS. HERBERT SNOW, LOS ANGELES

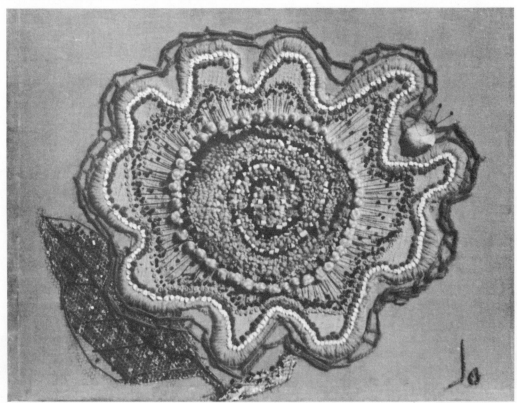

THERE'S ONE IN EVERY CROWD. Vesta Ward. Padded felt forms machine sewn to linen background. Surface stitching of heavy rug yarn with French knots and straight stitches only. COURTESY, ARTIST

SPACESHIP. Lee Erlin Snow. 9″ high, 12″ wide. French knots used in an abstract composition to increase the relief surface of the canvas stitch (*see* page 34).

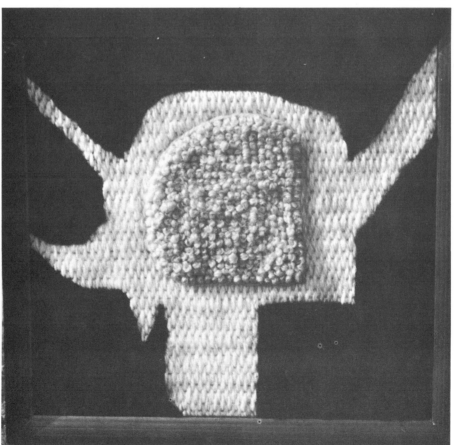

30

ST. BASILS, MOSCOW. Sherrill Kahn. All stitches illustrated have been combined to create a composition based on real and imaginary architectural forms.

NOT BY BREAD ALONE. Lee Erlin Snow. 16″ high, 20″ wide. Stitched letters very effectively use running, chain, and back stitches in many colors. In this case, an adage is combined with abstract biblical phrases.

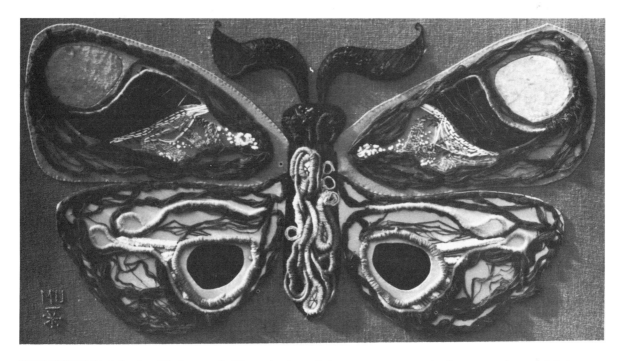

BUTTERFLY. Martha Underwood. Very thick and thin rug yarns couched to an appliqued fabric on a stretched backing have a visceral feeling. Heavy yarns or rope may be couched with the satin stitch for a greater bas-relief effect.

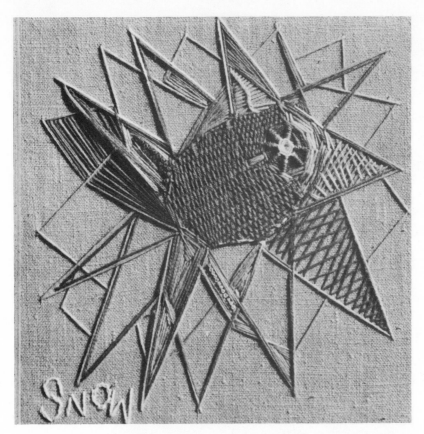

SQUAWKIN' BIRD. Lee Erlin Snow. 24″ square. Straight and herringbone stitches used as weaving on an orange linen background.

AUTUMN SUNBURST. Jeanette Cohen. Terry cloth and corduroy shapes on linen. Thick and thin yarns using long straight stitches, open ladder stitches, and French knots. PHOTO, VESTA WARD

FLAGS. Marilyn Pappas. Flannel flags, yarns, cording, and threads on linen backing. PHOTO, KLARA FARKAS

Canvas Stitching

Canvas work may be associated with needlepoint. It differs from embroidery or stitchery in that the stitch is made *into* a loosely woven piece of canvas backing and actually becomes part of the weave; it is not a surface decoration. However, stitchery may be combined with canvas work in an extremely creative, contemporary statement. By perfecting the simple canvas stitch illustrated on the following pages, and adding many of the stitches already demonstrated, canvas work becomes a challenging adaptation of two disciplines.

The work shown is most easily developed on pieces of canvas no more than 14 inches across so the hand can easily hold the material. Canvas work is not done on a frame so pieces may be folded and carried to be worked on at odd moments. This work is a marvelous time filler while waiting at the dentist's office, at meetings, or while watching TV with your household.

For canvas work, the entire surface of the backing is covered. You need a single mesh canvas with 12 or 14 meshes to the inch. A 3-ply Persian crewel yarn is recommended for a rich surface texture. (Most needlepoint employs a 2-ply yarn.) Use a #16, 17, or 18 blunt or sharp needlepoint needle to work into squares of the canvas.

For designs, simple shapes are best. Adapt words such as "yes" and "no" in abstract, stylized patterns. Use familiar forms such as a hand, heart, bird, bee, mushroom, or flower. You might cover the entire surface with the needlepoint stitch, then overlay the surface with stitchery. You might combine both on the canvas; or you might do stitchery alone into the canvas backing for another effect.

When canvas work pieces are small, there is no need to block them. In fact, whenever stitches are raised from a surface, blocking should be avoided.

MOTHER. Lee Erlin Snow. 10″ high, 14″ wide. Satin and back stitches are used to fill the meshes of the canvas backing. This is actually stitchery using needlepoint technique because the stitches are worked completely through the backing material.

HIM. Lee Erlin Snow. 8″ high, 10″ wide. Stitchery with canvas stitch (above) and painting (below) show the relationship that can be achieved in two media. Back stitches, French knots, and the canvas stitch are used. Colors are reds, hot pink, and yellow. Canvas work, and much stitchery, may also be interpreted in a painting. A painting may be an excellent subject for canvas designs even though executed on a much larger format. The painting measures 24″ x 30″.

36

Materials for canvas work include the canvas, single mesh with 12–14 meshes to the inch. Begin with a small piece about 12–14″ square. Any yarn will work, but 3-ply Persian yarn, available in scores of lush colors, will fill in the area quickly. Use 1–1½″ wide masking tape for the edges, scissors, blunt-end large-eyed tapestry or crewel-work needles, #16 tapestry needles, and waterproof felt-tip pen.

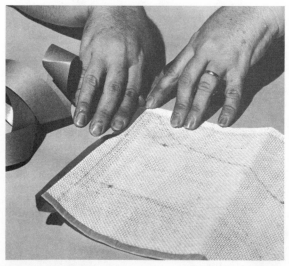

Mark off all edges of canvas equal to one-half the width of masking tape. Then mask all edges by bending tape over both sides of canvas to prevent edges from fraying.

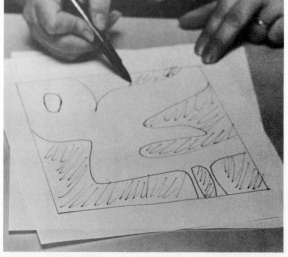

Many people design directly on the canvas, but a beginner would be wise to make his design on a piece of paper cut to the same size as canvas. (*See* "Red Angel" page 39.)

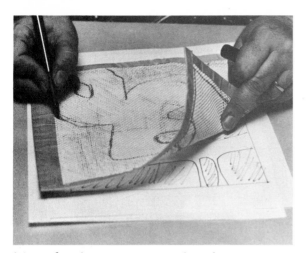

Transfer design to canvas by placing paper beneath canvas and drawing a pattern with a *waterproof* felt-tip pen so colors will not run if canvas is blocked.

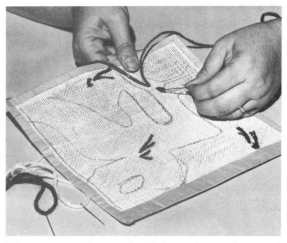

Place a sample stitch of the color to be used in each area for a reminder when you begin to work. Keep a couple of needles threaded with each color for odd waiting moments.

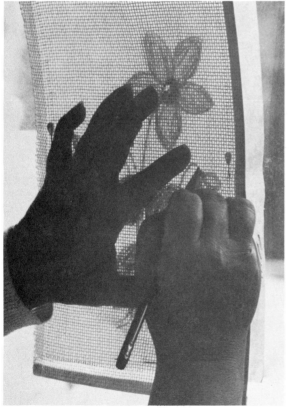

You can trace your pattern easily by putting the design on a window and letting the light show up the outlines.

Apply color tones with waterproof acrylic paints so you'll know which color to place in each area when you begin to work. Or paint a paper pattern. Design for "Morning Bird" by Esther Feldman.

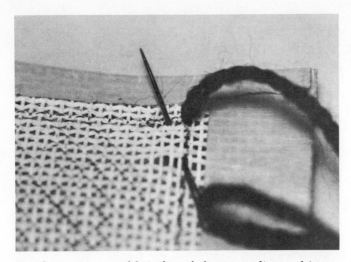

For first row, enter fabric from below at outline and insert needle five meshes up. Skip one mesh to begin next stitch.

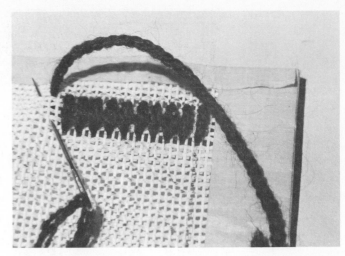

Continue the entire first row using every other mesh, five meshes high.

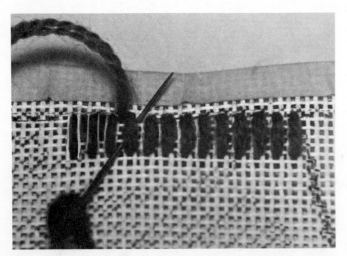

Now return and fill in the alternate blank mesh with a stitch only three meshes high on this row only. This establishes the pattern for the stitches to be worked into one another on subsequent rows.

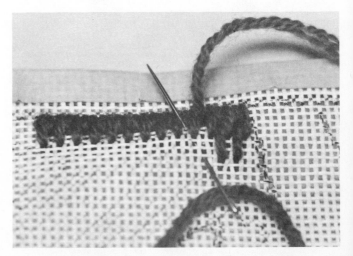

For *all* remaining area, work as on first row, making each stitch five meshes high and placing it every other mesh. Do not use any more than three mesh heights.

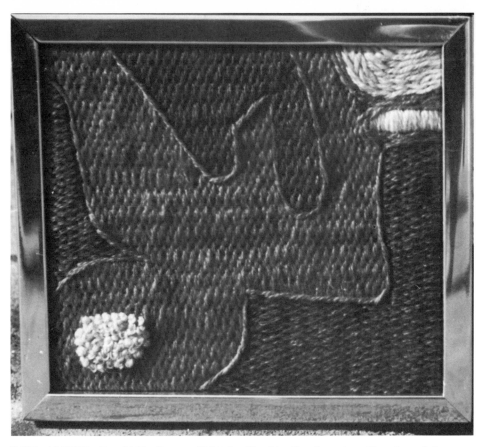

RED ANGEL. Lee Erlin Snow. 4″ high, 6″ wide. By changing direction of the canvas stitch you get another effect. The background is worked horizontally, and stitches for the angel are worked vertically. They are separated and outlined by a back stitch over the canvas stitches. French knot cluster adds another color and texture.

When you make a mistake, simply turn your canvas over, cut along the row of stitches, rip out, and begin again. Pulling out many stitches individually is too tedious.

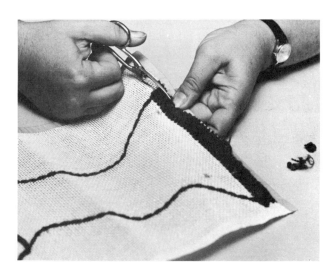

HOME IS HEART (detail of color photo facing page 56). Lee Erlin Snow. 24″ high, 24″ wide. Canvas stitch background worked in three shades of yellow has a tweed effect.

BLACK AND BROWN. Lee Erlin Snow. 7″ high, 9″ wide. Changing the directions of the canvas stitch results in a more varied surface texture. French knots and back stitch also are used on surface.

EXIT. Lee Erlin Snow. 6″ high, 12″ wide. Mostly satin and back stitches worked into the canvas backing. This is a satire on theater exit signs. Hot pinks on a purple background.

ANIMAL LANDSCAPE. Lee Erlin Snow. 4″ high, 10″ wide. Note the variety of stitches used, satin, canvas, straight, back, French knot. Some are for fill, others for outlining.

SUNFLOWERS. Carol Hansen Wagner. 5′ high, 3′ wide. Delicately colored silk organzas are overlaid and stitched to a sheer background fabric to result in a light ethereal feeling. COURTESY, THE EGG AND THE EYE, LOS ANGELES

3 Ideas, Colors, and Designs for Stitcheries

So far materials and methods have been introduced, along with examples, to whet your appetite for creative stitching. After making your sampler and learning the stitches that become part of your artistic vocabulary, the questions are: What to stitch? Where does one go for ideas? How does one apply them to stitchery? What colors should be used?

Ideas for Designs

Finding ideas is as easy as looking about the place where you are now sitting to discover some pattern that appeals to you. All you have to do to begin is to transfer the idea to fabric. If you are in your kitchen, open the refrigerator, take out an orange, a melon, a green pepper or a lemon. Cut it in half. There you have one of nature's most beautiful geometric designs—one that may easily be interpreted into a stitchery. Flowers, of course, are always popular subjects. Do not attempt to copy flowers photographically; rather, use nature's shapes, then edit and change lines and areas. Make your designs unique interpretations of nature's patterns.

There are few rules to creativity. No one can tell you how to express your views of an orange in colors and textures of yarn. Examples throughout the book should convince you that, with experimentation, trial, and error (which only means ripping out threads), your stitcheries can reveal your tastes, your likes and dislikes. They can

mirror any idea you have and be animated or quiet, stimulating or passive, bold or dispassionate. You can always achieve a beautiful composition, a symphony of design, texture, color, and mood.

You may prefer to work from pictures. Study magazine illustrations accompanying fiction and advertising. A still life of a dessert, for example, may have the outlines, shapes, forms, and colors you need to begin a stitchery. When seeking ideas, look for small details to expand into entire stitcheries. A drop of water on one petal of a rose can suggest the entire stitchery, with a bead as the water drop; there's no need to show the whole flower. Patterns on the bark of a tree and photos of objects taken microscopically often become more visually exciting than a familiar object treated realistically.

Take ideas from paintings: one artist uses threads as haphazardly as the dribbles on a Jackson Pollack painting to create a richly decorative and exciting surface. Details from etchings and other graphic arts, already interpreted in line and shape, can serve as design springboards. Study seed catalogues for flower shapes; use travel scenes, your children at play, your dreams, your memories; combine parts from many photos to make your own statement.

When specific objects escape you, work with abstract forms. Begin by placing a piece of yarn on a fabric in a doodlelike fashion. Attach it to the background, then fill in stitches in various directions and many colors. The first attempt may be a hodge-podge; by the second or third, you'll have a "feeling" for what stitches can do, how the threads and colors combine to make a unified composition. This doodle idea often is used by teachers as the first lesson following the sampler. It frees the student from tightly controlled realism. It teaches him to think of form for its own sake; subject identity is secondary.

Illustrations from children's books, religious books, record album covers, words, phrases, landscapes, movement, emotions (such as happiness, love, pleasure, displeasure)—all can be expressed with stitchery. Often a fabric itself will suggest a composition by the emotions it evokes or by its textures and shape.

If you like the idea of a doodle stitchery, you might practice scribbling free-form designs on paper. Drawings may be as sketchy as those of Lee Snow; or as detailed as those of Martha Underwood. It doesn't matter so long as you are able to interpret them and think of them as ideas for stitcheries.

Many artists have devised other ways to help create a design. Fabrics may be tie-dyed and bleached, as shown on the following pages. Cut-out paper shapes can help you relate fabrics to one another. You might also crease the fabric in many directions, then work stitches where the creases made shapes. You can use any device you like to stimulate patterns.

So far this chapter has emphasized the tremendous freedom inherent in the act of creating stitcheries. That is as it should be. There are no rules, no hard and fast do's and don'ts, no one way to approach this exciting art form.

DOODLE STITCHERY. To experiment with freedom of design, wiggle a heavy thread in a doodlelike fashion on a backing, couch it, and fill in with different color threads and stitches.

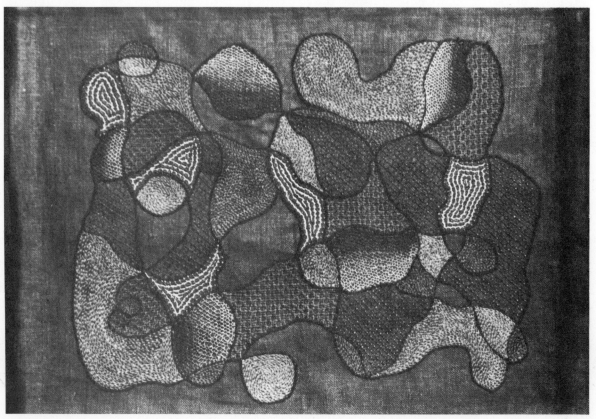

Close up view of a Bird of Paradise with pointed leaves may easily be interpreted into a realistic or abstract stitchery.

Spurs and horseshoes suggest stars and other forms that could inspire patterns for a wall hanging.

This cut papaya melon in brilliant orange yellows could be the basis for a stitchery. Outlines could be back stitched; the meaty parts of the melon, satin stitched; black seeds, French knots over a center of grouped chain stitches.

Border designs, interior patterns, and complete stitcheries could be composed from elements taken from the worn surfaces of ancient stone sculptures. Erosion results in an abstract feeling.

Root forms can inspire the imagination. Observe designs and shapes of petals, stones, and even muck on water. PHOTO, GAR GREENE

The patterns and textures of wood, stone, and metal may be imagined as a composition. One could use only a detail of this photo or the entire piece for a stitchery.

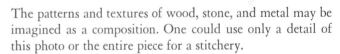

Color

Color is an exciting and important characteristic of contemporary stitchery. Yarns and fabrics are so varied in their hues, values, and intensities that a yarn counter is a veritable potpourri of color delight—a delight that is easily transferable to artistic expression.

It is important to control use of color so that you are not completely carried away. You can plan and select a scheme by experimenting with color relationships of yarns much more easily than the painter can work with his pigments. You may simply place skeins of yarns and threads next to each other until you find a pleasing combination.

It is important to play with yarns when they are still in skeins to see how they complement or contrast with one another. Sometimes two skeins of one color but of different values will not look well together: two greens not of the same family, for example, may distort the color of each

other when placed together. And such clashes can completely ruin the effect being planned. Therefore it is always important to juxtapose colors and to examine their relationships to each other and to the backing fabric.

You may also plan color schemes by selecting colors in a piece of drapery fabric, a painting, or a dress. Then use them in a similar relationship.

One may think of color relationships as a painter does; in terms of "dominance," "subordination," and "accent." This old rule insists that one color is the most important, or dominant. The second color is used in a subordinate role; the third color for accents.

Once you decide on colors, snip short pieces of the fabrics or yarn and stitch or pin them in sections of your design to decide where they should go.

Color combinations are myriad. You might try a combination of monochromatic colors: one color with variations of value and intensity; of complementary colors

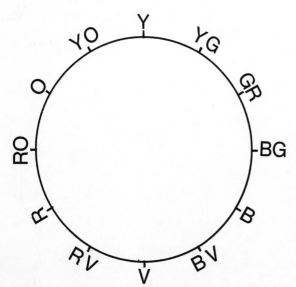

Primary colors, yellow, blue, and red, are the sources of all other colors. The binary colors, green, orange, and violet, are made by mixing together the primary colors next to each other.

Complementary colors are those directly opposite each other on the color wheel. Near-complementary colors harmonize effectively with each other.

Color value is the difference between light and dark, such as between light or dark green. Color intensity is the brightness or grayness of a color.

IN THE TROUGH OF THE SEA. Albert Pinkham Ryder. Oil on canvas (detail). Details of paintings offer another source for composition ideas. They should be updated and combined with original ideas for more expressive and innovative stitcheries. COURTESY, ART INSTITUTE OF CHICAGO

SUNDAY AFTERNOON AT LA GRANDE JATTE. Georges Seurat. Oil on canvas (detail). COURTESY, ART INSTITUTE OF CHICAGO

HOMAGE TO STUART DAVIS. Dona Meilach. Composition adapted from a painting. Composed of yarn—using four strands at once in a tapestry needle and filling with the satin stitch.

(those opposite each other on the color wheel can also be varied with tints, tones, and shades—yellows with violets, greens with reds, etc.). You could work with related colors: those next to each other on the color wheel (yellows with greens and oranges). Think in terms of warm and cool colors also. The warm colors—reds, oranges, and yellows—can be interworked with subordinated and accent colors—blues and greens.

Color is, essentially, a quality you learn to feel as you work with it. Like all other "rules" in this book, there are no rules for color use. Try what you like and continue to try new combinations. If something doesn't please you, simply try something else until you are satisfied.

Sketches may be made quickly at odd moments of inspiration. Merely indicate colors, then work up the stitchery using the idea presented. Lee Erlin Snow.

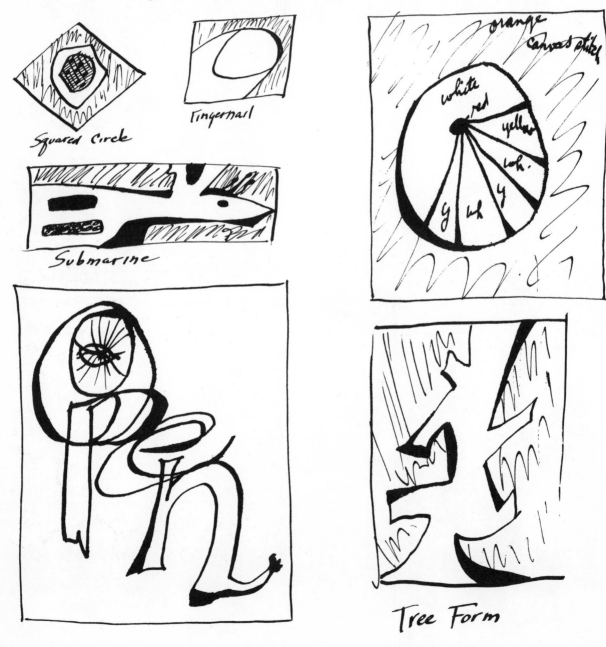

Or sketches may be carefully drawn before interpreting them in fabrics. Sketches by Martha Underwood, inspired by fruits and vegetables, are developed in the designs below.

Martha Underwood's final stitcheries are usually different from her drawings, and this is perfectly understandable. It isn't necessary to interpret a pencil sketch exactly in fabric, and there is no reason to do so. *A sketch is an idea, not the finished work.*

50

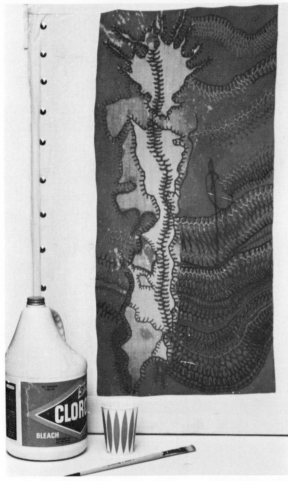

Designing with Bleach

Henry Stahmer has developed a unique way to create abstract designs. He stretches a washable cotton or colored linen fabric onto a frame. Here he has sewn a colored rectangle to a piece of muslin and stretched it over a frame. The muslin absorbs much of the pull so that the backing fabric is not weakened. Later, he will separate the backing from the muslin cloth to frame it. Then, using a fabric bleach, he simply "paints out" some of the color quickly, using first a one-half bleach and one-half water solution, then straight bleach. When blurry shapes result, he removes the fabric from the frame and washes it several times to remove all the bleach. He uses the subtle shadings for shapes to develop his stitcheries, perhaps placing darker colors on the bleached portions, lighter colors on the original fabric color. He blends and ties tones together with the threads used. Details below.

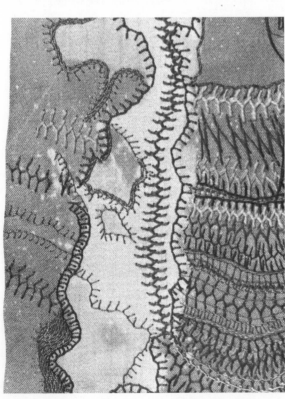

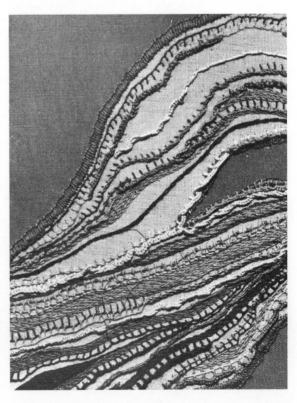

FIREBALL (detail of stitchery on page 20). Henry Stahmer. Observe how the fabric is shaded and the stitches used to pull color areas together.

BLACK BLEACHED. Henry Stahmer. When bleaching, test a scrap of fabric first to be sure color will bleach.

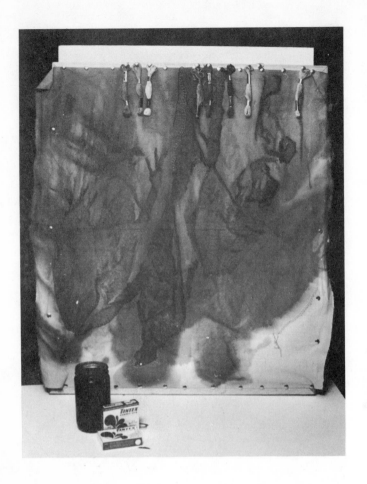

Designing with Dyes

The use of dyes for tinting fabric is an ancient technique. Used with modern stitchery concepts, dyed fabrics can stimulate an entire range of subtle compositions and blends.

One method used by Henry Stahmer consists of tacking a white cotton or linen fabric to a frame, diluting the dyes, then letting them dribble across the surface of the fabric by twisting and turning the material from side to side so that it streaks. This process shows the hues and graduated tones that result (see detail below). Depending upon the dyes used and the color of the base fabric, embroidery threads are selected. Stahmer tacks skeins of thread to the surface of the backing to see how tones will work together when completed.

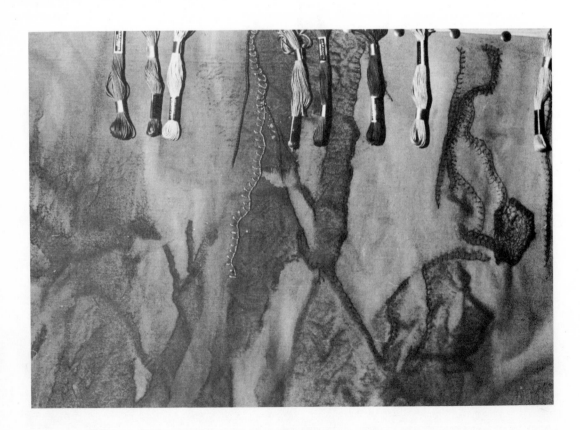

Tie-dying and batik are other means of achieving tinted fabric backgrounds for abstract stitchery compositions. Fabric at right has been tie-dyed with blues.

Below, tie-dying, here used with bleach. Handfuls of green cotton, pretested to be sure they will bleach, are tied up, using a cord dipped in melted paraffin. The fabric is allowed to remain in the bleach for several minutes, depending on weave, weight of fabric, and effect desired. It is then washed to remove the bleach, and a subtle "print" results.

Experiment with a scrap of fabric to determine the time it takes for bleaching. In the photo above, a white fabric was treated with blue dyes in the same manner.

THE ICY QUILT OF DEEP DECEMBER. Helen Richards. 28″ high, 34″ wide. Inspired by Jack Frost on a window pane. Background of black raw silk with cheesecloth shredded and pulled, unraveled knitted pieces, slub yarns, rayons and wools, with stitchery. COURTESY, ARTIST

RUSSIA. Charlotte Patera. 14½″ high, 23″ wide. Design inspired by an illustration in the children's book *BABA YAGA*. Various colored wool yarns on an orange rayon linen backing. PHOTO, GEORGE RIEKMAN

IN MY GRANDFATHER'S HOUSE. Bess Powell. 24″ high, 16″ wide. Applique and stitches on linen background trace the artist's memories of her childhood in Russia. Samovar, stove, fruitful fields, and grandfather.

GIRL WITH MIRROR. Tina Krythe. 50″ high, 36″ wide. Design suggested by watching her daughter primp before a mirror.

GIRL IN THE GARDEN. Esther Feldman. 40″ high, 24″ wide. Flowers, always a favorite for designing, are given an additional concept by having the girl's figure "behind" them. Upholstery fabric background with large variety of stitches done in an assortment of thick and thin yarns.

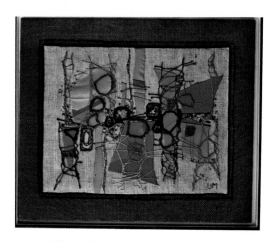

Silks and Laces, Martha Underwood.

Home Is Heart, Lee Erlin Snow.

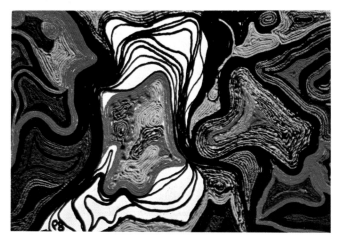

Yarn Painting (detail), Estelle Carlson.

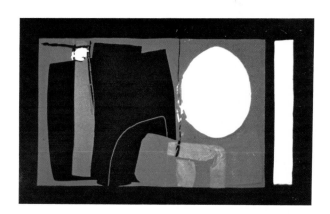

Universal, Jeanne Boardman.

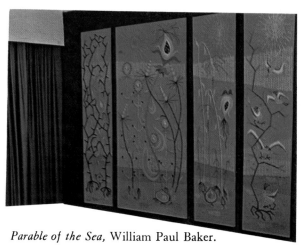

Parable of the Sea, William Paul Baker.

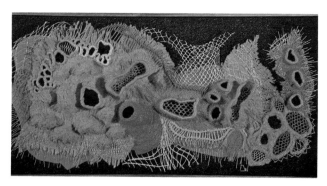

Mexicana Rosa, Evelyn Svec Ward.

Silks and Laces. Martha Underwood. 24″ high, 28″ wide. Silk applique on linen mounted on gold upholstery fabric. Weaving yarns stitched over, but not through, the silks.   COURTESY, ARTIST

Home Is Heart. Lee Erlin Snow. 24″ square. Canvas work with stitchery in bold color yarns.
                                        PHOTO, DONA MEILACH

Yarn Painting (detail). Estelle Carlson. Various sizes, colors and textures of yarns stitched to a backing in free form movement much as paint is drippled onto a canvas.   COURTESY, ARTIST

Universal. Jeanne Boardman. 18″ high, 24″ wide. Fabric collage as an interpretation of hard-edge painting.   COURTESY, ARTIST

Parable of the Sea. William Paul Baker. Sheer fabric with stitchery framed and used as a room divider.   COURTESY, ARTIST

Mexicana Rosa. Evelyn Svec Ward. 11″ high, 21″ wide. Varieties of threads and stitches with burlap, netting, and felt on wool. Detached stitches create raised areas.   PHOTO, WILLIAM E. WARD

UNTITLED. Darryl Groover. 36″ high, 24″ wide. Various black and white dotted fabrics and solid fabrics were stitched onto a fabric background in a collage method, the fabrics suggesting the design. PHOTOGRAPHED AT CANYON GALLERY II, LOS ANGELES

58

DESIGN. Frances Robinson. Black silk, machine
stitchery in white, pale blue, brown, and purple.
COURTESY, THE COOPER UNION MUSEUM, NEW YORK

CLAPBOARD HOUSE. Harlene Schwartz. 31" high, 21" wide. A home with a kitten at the door, a mailbox, and cut pieces of doilies for flowers is executed on a blue wool background. The façade is white with red roof. Touches of lace and doilies in the windows and reds in the window flowers all add to the nostalgic, homey quality of this stitchery. Mounted on fiberboard for backing before framing.

PHOTO, BRENT LOWENSOHN

FRUITFUL TREE. Blanche Carstenson. 25″ high, 21″ wide. Threads and hand-woven fabrics on a yellow cotton backing. Assorted threads are handled in much the same manner as a painter uses paints. Only a few types of stitches are used; notice that the thick wool yarns framing the piece are couched with a blanket stitch in a contrasting thread. COURTESY, ARTIST

4   Multiple Fabrics

Contemporary stitchery owes much of its excitement to the infinite combinations of fabrics possible. In the past, surface decoration of one fabric with another was essentially done by applique painstakingly blindstitched. Edges of the appliqued materials were carefully turned under so that no raw edges would show, no areas fray. This treatment was important for useful objects that had to take daily wear and washings. For the art object, such applique is still used, along with other types of rich surface decoration in a more expressive, loose, rough, contemporary manner.

Given the multiple fabrics employed in modern stitcheries, neatly blindstitched edges are no longer essential. In addition to rough, shaggy, raveled treatment of edges, one also discovers materials padded so that they protrude from the picture surface, perhaps even hang beyond it. Frequently, there are so many materials heaped on a backing that the work resembles a sculptured relief. High and low surfaces catch changing light and shadow; they are as ingeniously planned as the friezes on the Parthenon. Others are frankly done as stitchery sculpture in a three dimensional statement meant to be viewed from all around.

Multiple fabric stitcheries can be inventive, experimental, and innovative. There are no limits to the materials one can use: wools, silks, nets, chiffons, velvets, tie-dyed cottons, crocheted, knotted, and knitted parts, lace, burlap, etc. Nor are stitcheries confined to fabrics alone. Many stitcheries include beads, buttons, ceramics, pasta, furs, leather, mirrors, feathers, pods, wood, and more—for greater visual and tactile experience.

The intrepid stitcher is like a pack rat, storing scraps and bits of miscellany that promise an animated dimension to a planned wall hanging. He saves pieces of fabrics that others might throw away, often salvaging discards. He may so covet a pure silk blouse for its sheer beauty of fabric that he asks the wearer to save it for him when she tires of it. He is attuned to the

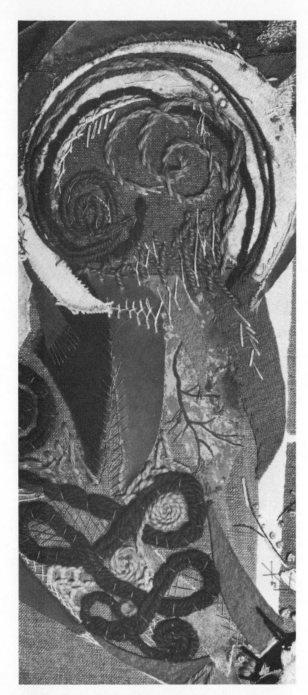

BIRD FOR JENNIFER (detail). Jettie Penraat.
Collage stitchery using a variety of fabrics and yarns.
Linen backing stretched over a wood frame. COUR-
TESY, ARTIST

beauty of weaves, dyes, patterns, light on the surface of a material, the complete range of fabrics and their potential relationship to one another. The appreciation of the qualities of materials and of their possibilities of design is not something one achieves overnight or in five quick lessons. It is an appreciation that is learned and savored as one works.

If your first designs are a struggle, that is as it should be. In time, you will nurture the sixth sense that artists gradually develop by contact with their materials and visions. Your first stitcheries can be beautiful and successful, but subsequent ones eventually will be more so.

Blanche Carstenson explains that she uses very few types of stitches, but she does employ a great variety of threads and fabrics. "If I think of stitches," she says, "I get embroidery. So I use fabric as collage and think of my threads as paint."

To begin work with multiple fabrics,

cut out or drape fabrics and materials in interesting and stimulating color relations, then stitch them to the background. Your stitchery sampler taught you how to use stitches; now you might like to add fabrics to the same sampler or to a new one. Applique different fabrics, first with the running stitch, then with other stitches. You will quickly learn that stitches are both the means of attaching fabrics to the surface and a decorative addition that is made to the surface.

Include both carefully tucked-under edges and shaggy edges, and observe the different effect of each. You might purposely pull threads along the edge of a fabric for a fringed appearance. As you study examples, learn to "see" how materials are handled, as well as learn to understand the designs and subjects presented. Looking at stitcheries and the manner in which they have been done is the best stimulus for applying your own ideas to fabrics.

BOAT WITH WHEELS GOING NOWHERE (detail). Ronald M. Rolfe. Colored felt machine appliques with some hand stitching.

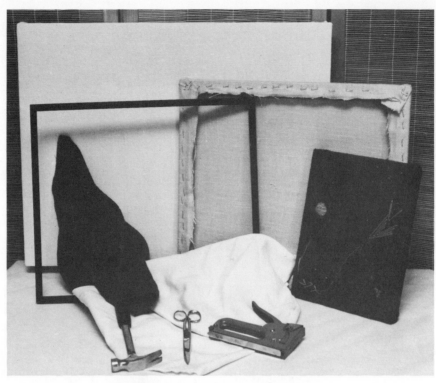

Working on a Framed Backing

Making your own framed backing is very easy. Begin with a sturdy narrow frame; scrap frames will do, it isn't necessary to buy stretcher bars. Thick or wide moldings prevent you from working to the edge of your composition. You may prefer to use the stretched fabric edge as the only frame. Materials include frame, backing fabric, stapler, scissors, and hammer.

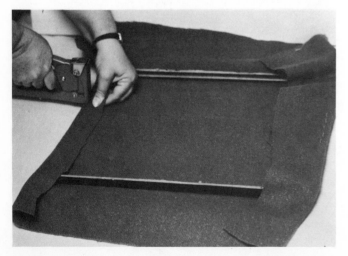

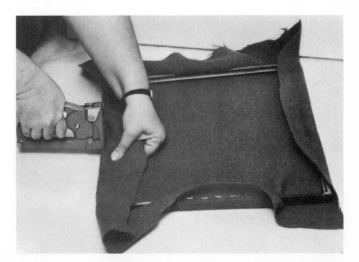

Measure fabric by setting frame on top of it, allowing enough material on all sides for the hand to pull it taut. Set frame on fabric in direction of weave, not diagonally to it. Staple *center only* of fabric on one side, then pull from center on opposite side and staple. The trick is to stretch until it is drum tight.

Now do the same to the third and fourth sides. Always work opposite sides and combine pulling and stapling, working to about one inch of each corner. A linen or upholstery fabric is best for backing. Shown is an upholstery fabric that will remain quite taut while working.

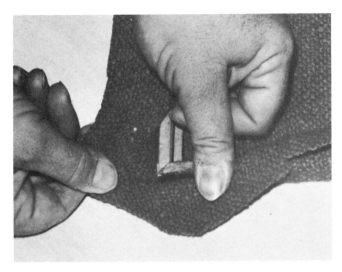

Next, trim the fabric at the corner, allowing about a two-inch edge so that the folds you make won't be too bulky. Pull the center corner taut.

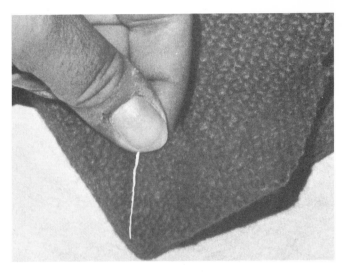

Make two or three tiny folds rather than one large mitered fold. Place the first fold to one side of the corner and staple.

Make a second fold next to the first and then a third fold so the outside corner is neatly pulled over the edge of frame and inside accumulation of fabric is not too bulky. Repeat this on all four corners, always pulling the fabric taut before stapling. If any staples protrude, hammer them down so they don't catch on your clothes as you work.

Finish stapling the fabric to corner. Staples should be quite close to one another. Trim the inside edge of the fabric. When the stitchery is completed, a linen or cotton material may be stitched or stapled to back frame edge for a neater finish. Often, no additional framing is necessary when this method is used.

Many people prefer to work stitcheries on frames with the base materials held taut. (This is the same principle as using an embroidery hoop except the larger surface enables you to develop your work in a freer manner. Hoops tend to stretch a fabric out of shape.) With a tautly held base fabric, your attached fabrics will lay better. Stitches applied to taut fabric tend to pull less than when the fabric is held loosely.

Use your sewing machine for attaching fabrics and for adding design touches to the work. Remember, there are no rules, no blueprints for contemporary stitchery. There is no one "best way" of working. No two people using the same fabrics will create the same finished work. No two projects will be exactly alike; each must be pondered for the best way to approach and conclude the work. Techniques offered are shortcuts. Develop your own methods. One artist plans large stitcheries by spreading and pinning the backing fabric directly to the rug on her floor, then pinning other materials and threads to that.

Stitcheries may also be framed as you frame a picture. If a stitchery is to be mounted on a backing board, the bottom threads should not have large knots—perhaps no knots at all—when a large knot is placed against a backing board, it tends to put a lump through to the face of the stitchery. If possible, then, work without knotting and instead leave several inches of thread at the back. These lengths may be woven among other threads.

Finished stitcheries may be hung from rods. Backing treatment will be determined by the type of materials, edges desired, and the way the piece is hung. For a more finished hanging, line the back of the stitchery to cover the array of threads. Sew the lining to the stitchery all around the edges, hemming where necessary. Place several tack threads at intervals in the inner part of the stitchery to hold lining and base fabric together. A rod may go through the top hem or be suspended by fabric or ribbon.

Stitcheries should be sprayed with a fabric guard to prevent them from absorbing dust and grease. Glass framing is usually unsatisfactory because it tends to squash the fabric, and thereby the values of the textures and surfaces are minimized.

A good working position is to place the top of frame against a table and the bottom in your lap, thus allowing ample space to pull needle in and out.

Directions for Blindstitching

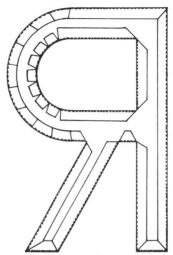

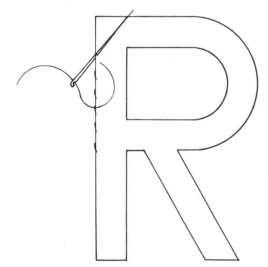

A. Design the pattern piece on applique fabric. Mark a seam allowance all around pattern piece. Machine stitch on pattern outline (dotted line) for neat turning edge. Carefully cut out fabric on seam allowance line. Remember that the design will be reversed when attached.

B. Clip into seam allowance on all edges and at corners. On curved edges make tiny slits at angles to the stitching. Turn in seam allowance and machine stitching so that it will not show when reversed. Press.

C. Pin and then baste fabric applique piece in place. Use tiny invisible stitches for true blindstitching. The applique might also be attached with large, obvious stitches.

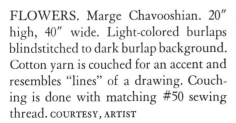

FLOWERS. Marge Chavooshian. 20″ high, 40″ wide. Light-colored burlaps blindstitched to dark burlap background. Cotton yarn is couched for an accent and resembles "lines" of a drawing. Couching is done with matching #50 sewing thread. COURTESY, ARTIST

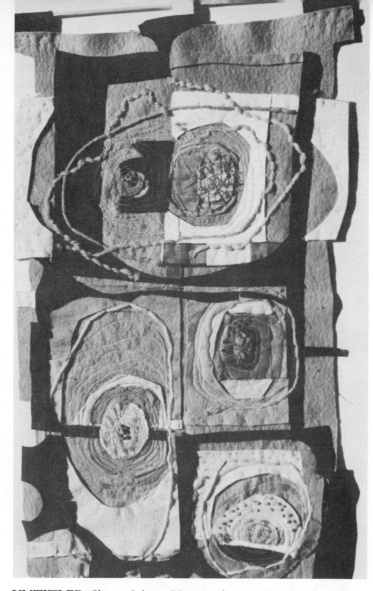

UNTITLED. Sherry Schrut. Hanging banner, hand and machine appliqued on felt and wool. COURTESY, ARTIST

BLACKBIRD TREE. Joan Orme. 18″ high, 30″ wide. Cotton, felt, and velvet. COURTESY, ARTIST

FOREST FLOWERS. Martha Underwood. 4½′ high, 5′ wide. Applique with stitchery. Black wool flannel and upholstery materials appliqued to an upholstery fabric. Wool yarns of many weights are stitched. Yarn is looped loosely around the large flowers. COURTESY, ARTIST

PRIMITIF. Charlotte Patera. 18″ high, 24″ wide. Ocher, olive, and brown broadcloth shapes appliqued to an off-white kettle-cloth. Rick-rack edges. PHOTO, GEORGE RIEKMAN

"YES, VIRGINIA . . ." Alma Lesch. 38" high, 24" wide. Fabric collage with velvet dress, kerchief, lace collar, fan, book, and stitchery on linen. COURTESY, ARTIST

SANTA PRISCA. Jeanne Dunlap. 36" high, 22" wide. Hot pinks, orange, cerise, and black felt with old doilies, netting, and organza on off-white linen. COLLECTION: MR. AND MRS. JOSEPH M. HENNINGER, PACIFIC PALISADES, CALIFORNIA

MEMORIAL. Lee Erlin Snow. 20″ high, 30″ wide. Background cut from the last wool coat her father gave her before he died. Raised area, brown textured fabric from dress she wore to his funeral. Butterfly shape and bee symbolize life on earth.

THE BLACKS AND THE REDS. Lee Erlin Snow. 16″ high, 20″ wide. Edges are purposely left rough and shaggy. Very simple stitches used to hold applique to linen backing. Feathers and beads. Plain sewing thread used.

NIGHTSCAPE: WINTER. Gary Barlow. Hand and machine applique with stitchery. COURTESY, ARTIST

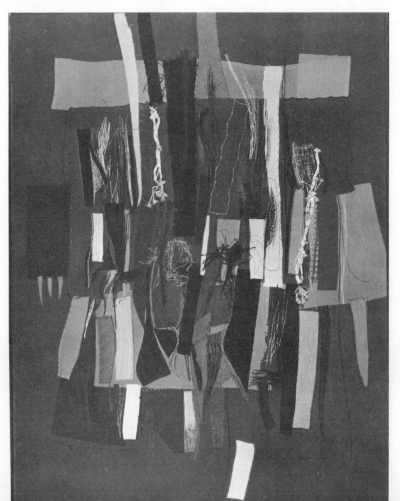

EAST, EAST. Gary Barlow. Applique and stitchery. COURTESY, ARTIST

CHRYSANTHEMUM. Ted Ball. Cotton applique of a flower abstracted. PHOTO, BOB LOPEZ

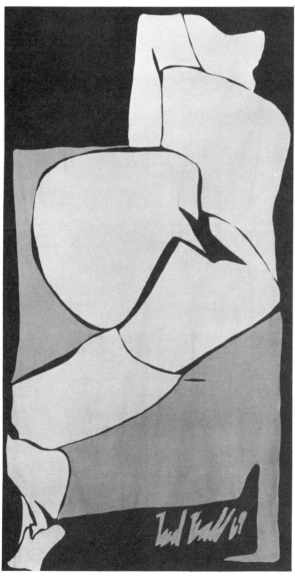

NUDE. Ted Ball. Cotton applique floor-to-ceiling hanging is abstract with a monumental feeling. PHOTO, BOB LOPEZ

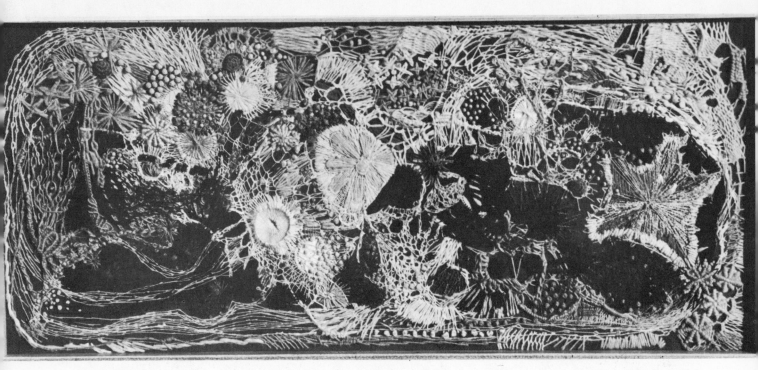

TIDE POOL. Esther Feldman. 18″ high, 24″ wide. Many different stitches plus macrame and needle weaving on background of upholstery fabric.

TIDE POOL (detail). Esther Feldman. A sea shell is stitched directly to fabric.

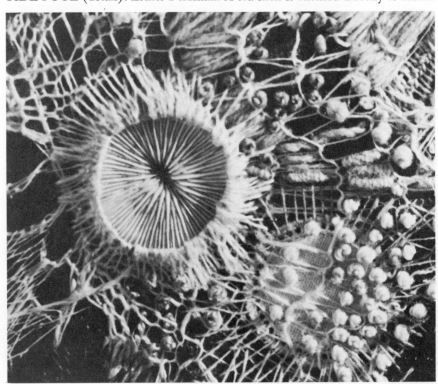

THE EDGE OF THE SEA. Bets Ramsey. 30″ high, 50″ wide. A landscape created from patches of blues, greens, and tan sheer organdy stitched on linen. Net, nylon yarn, and machine stitching. COURTESY, ARTIST

SUNNY LANDSCAPE. Sherrill Kahn. 24″ high, 30″ wide. Variety of fabrics machine and hand appliqued.

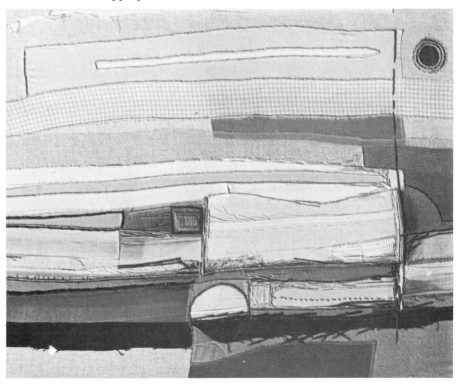

SHADES OF MEXICO. Lee Erlin Snow. 16″ high, 20″ wide. Frayed edges emphasized for texture and composition.

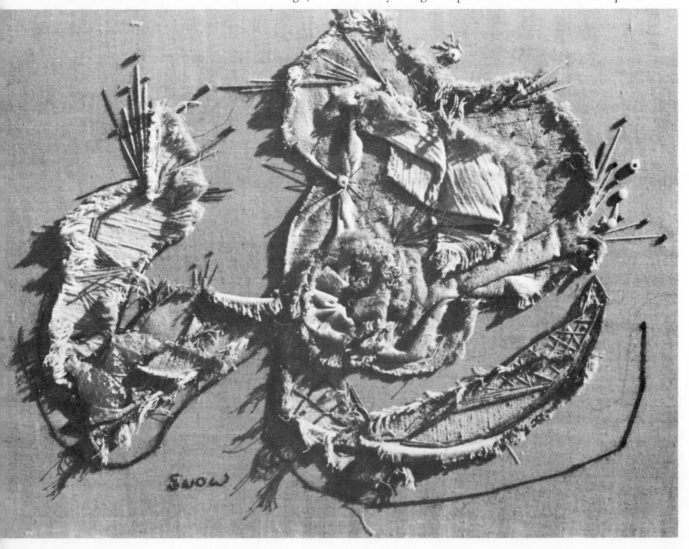

LOVE IS LIFE. Berni Gorski. 30″ diameter. Batiked fabric used for letters and bits of old lace are appliqued. Stitchery over all on a raw silk backing stretched over plywood. PHOTO, HENRY GORSKI

AMERICAN BOY. Susan H. Brown. 21″ high, 25″ wide. An old pair of blue jeans, including pockets, belts, patches, and rips, appliqued with stitchery on a framed fabric. COURTESY, ARTIST

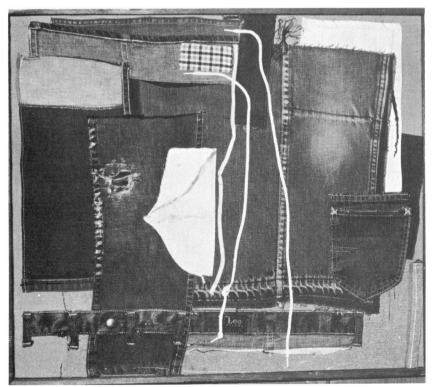

78

ANGRY BIRD. Lucille Brokaw. 21″ high, 26″ wide. Fabric collage, oil painting, and stitchery on a piece of fabric mounted on a cut wood backing. COURTESY, ARTIST

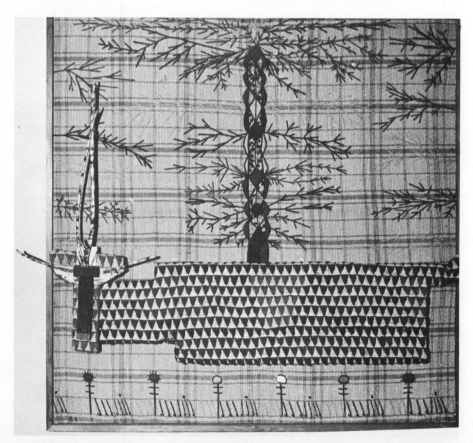

RAIBAB ANTELOPE. Lucille Brokaw. 50″ high, 52″ wide. Collage and stitchery, termed "cousage" by the artist, consists of overlaid pieces of wood covered with fabric and stitched. Zodiac symbols are interpreted in stitchery. COURTESY, ARTIST

UNTITLED. Darryl Groover. A woven
swatch stitched to linen backing contributes
to the rough-textured, rugged appearance.
PHOTOGRAPHED AT CANYON GALLERY II, LOS
ANGELES

UKIYO. Pamela Stearns. 18½″ high, 25″
wide. Wool, linen, and silk yarns on cotton.
Stitchery mounted on panel of stained
wood. Some applique and block printing.
PHOTO, GEORGE DIPPLE

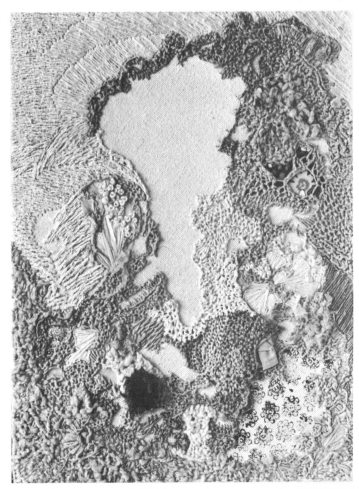

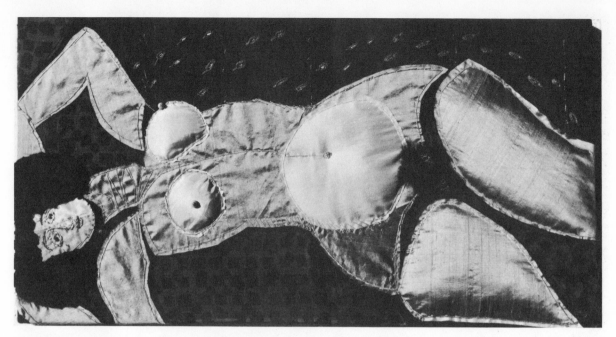

BRONZE NUDE. Lee Erlin Snow. 14″ high, 22″ wide. Silks and shimmering surfaced fabrics in bronze shades. Some areas stuffed for sculptural three-dimensional effect. PHOTO, HELFANT

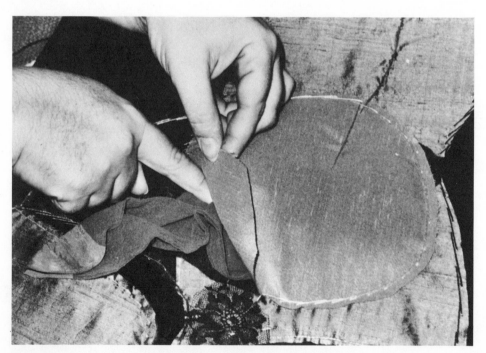

In addition to using fabrics in the manner of collage, greater surface relief may be achieved by stuffing portions of the work. Simply cut a shape larger than the area to be covered to allow for the raised fabric. Pin to the area to be stuffed.

Using desired stitches, sew about three-fourths of the shape to the backing, allowing enough room to work in your stuffing material. Old nylon stockings are used here but any soft fabrics or leftover yarn may be used. In long, deep areas, push stuffing into shape with a knitting needle or other long instrument. Then finish the stitching.

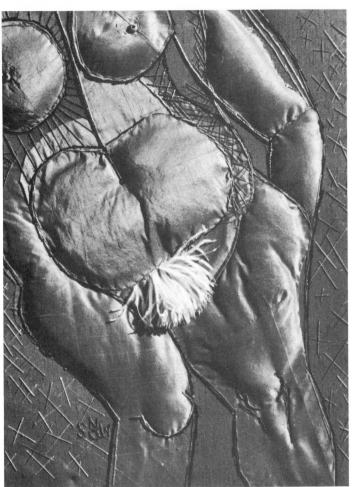

LA PLUME DE MA TANTE. 16″ high, 20″ wide. Lee Erlin Snow. Stuffed applique with stitchery. The pure silk fabric has an appealing shimmer as it catches lights and shadows. Hot pinks and reds.

BUT, ALL WAYS A LADY. 16″ high, 20″ wide. Lee Erlin Snow. Lavender pure silk body stuffed and appliqued on purple upholstery background, with stitchery. Peacock feather headdress extends beyond picture plane.

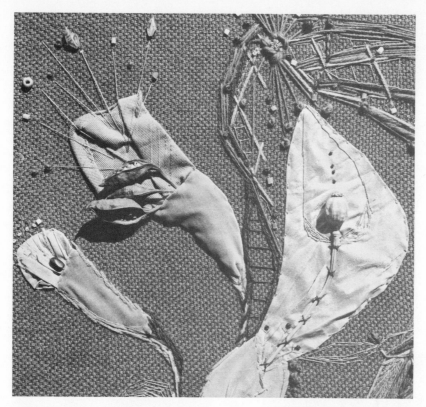

PODS (detail). Lee Erlin Snow. Flower parts of various fabrics may be stuffed also. Here, draped velvet is padded to give the illusion and reality of depth, from which real dried pods are sprouting.

TIGER. Sherly Sacks. Stuffed and stitched.

THE IRONY OF TRUCK AND SONG. Anita Gorr. Wool yarn on burlap backing stretched over a wood frame. Solid portions are padded canvas with details painted with acrylics. Some rug hooking. COLLECTION: MRS. ROBERT H. HUNTOON, SYOSSET, NEW YORK

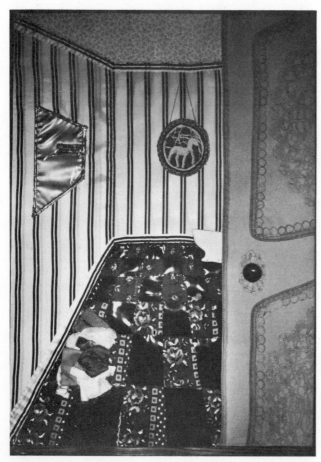

THOUGHTS. Harlene Schwartz. 25″ high, 19″ wide. Tremendous perspective achieved. Mirror is clear plastic over gray satin to give a glossy look.

PHOTO, BRENT LOWENSOHN

CIRCLES. Anna M. Sunnergren. 5′ high, 3′ wide. Silk fabrics appliqued with combination machine and hand stitching. COURTESY, ARTIST

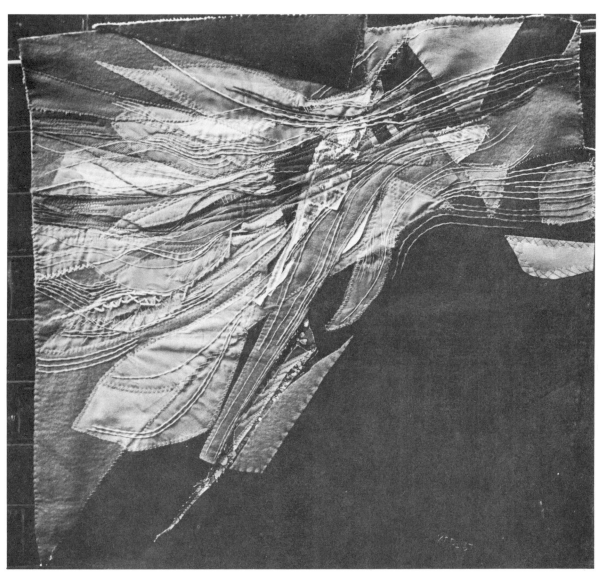

NIGHTSONG. Kristina Friberg. 22″ square. Felt, cotton, leather, and organdy. Hand and machine stitchery.
PHOTO, HASSE PERSSON

Ecclesiastical subjects are popular for stitchery.

GO AND BE RECONCILED. Norman Laliberte. COURTESY, THE UNIVERSITY OF CHICAGO

HEBREW SYMBOLS. Blanche Carstenson. 5' high, 4' wide. Collage on Belgian linen with many types of threads using simple stitches. COURTESY, ARTIST

CATHEDRAL. Ronald M. Rolfe. 45″ high, 29″ wide. Felt, padded sheer cotton for stained window effect. Monks cloth backing. Machine and hand stitchery with crewel wool yarn and cotton floss.

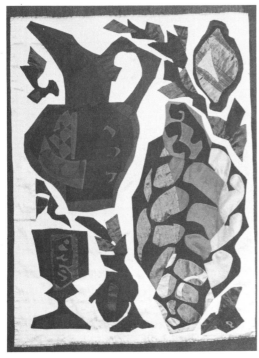

SUDA (detail). Sophia Adler. Applique wall hanging for a Temple with symbols from stories of the Bible. COURTESY, ARTIST

THE MAGICAL GARDEN. Lillian Delevoryas. 29″ high, 22″ wide. Applique with many textured fabrics.
COURTESY, ARTIST

Across the Street, Max Daches.

The U.S. and Harper Hill, Marilyn Pappas.

Inside—Outside, Harlene Schwartz.

The Metal Age, Alpha Salveson.

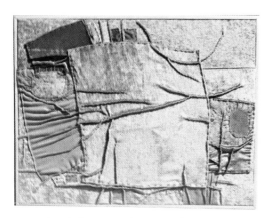

Abstraction in Velvet, Josephine Diggs.

Quarry #2, Gary Barlow.

Across the Street. Max Daches. Nostalgic childhood scene created with machine embroidery.

COURTESY, ARTIST

The U.S. and Harper Hill. Marilyn Pappas. 48″ high, 60″ wide. Fabric collage using army uniform parts, yarns, fabric trims, scraps, and a screen print on a linen backing.

COURTESY, ARTIST

Inside—Outside. Harlene Schwartz. 25″ square. Three dimensional effect achieved on a flat surface with fabrics, trims, and objects.

COURTESY, ARTIST

The Metal Age. Alpha Salveson. 36″ high, 24″ wide. Cut work of heavy black pellon on backing of yellow ocher wool. Yarns stitched in cut-out areas range from heavy spun to lightweight silk threads.

COURTESY, ARTIST

Abstraction in Velvet. Josephine Diggs. 22″ high, 30″ wide. Worn velvet upholstery fabric cut and stitched. Pieces appliqued so fabric nap changes direction for different light effect.

COURTESY, ARTIST

Quarry #2. Gary Barlow. Colored cottons and rayons appliqued using both trim and frayed edges.

COURTESY, ARTIST

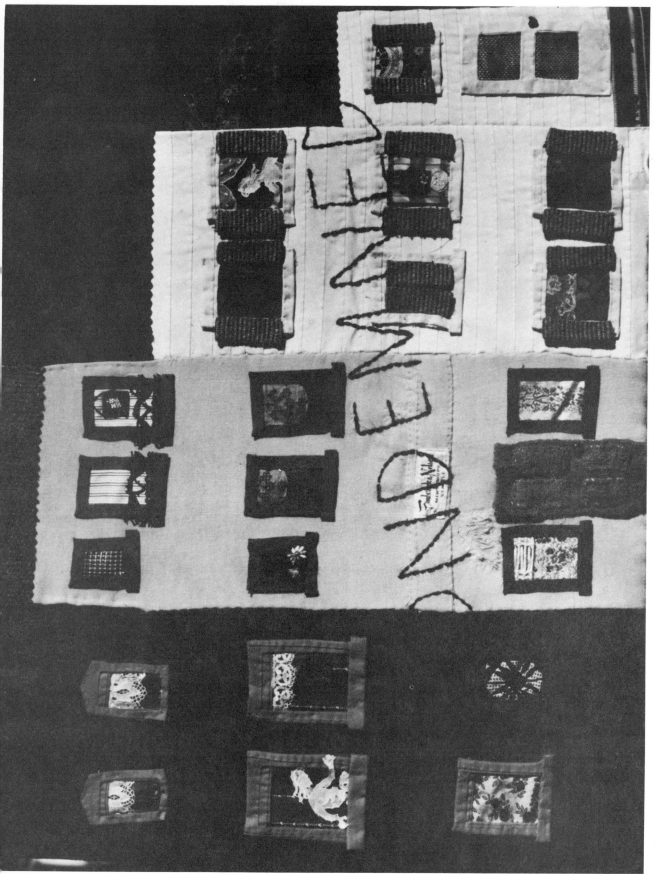

CONDEMNED. Harlene Schwartz. 25″ high, 19″ wide. Social commentary can be achieved in stitchery as it can in other art media. COLLECTION: MR. & MRS. JERRY LECHAY, STUDIO CITY. PHOTO, BRENT LOWENSOHN

The San Blas Indians of Panama are known for their reverse cutting applique. Rather than place one piece of fabric on top of another and stitch them together, they use four or more layers of fabric under one another. They cut through the layers and fold back the edges of one to reveal those beneath. It's a complicated, time-consuming technique that has been greatly updated by modern stitchers. COLLECTION: MR. & MRS. HERBERT SNOW

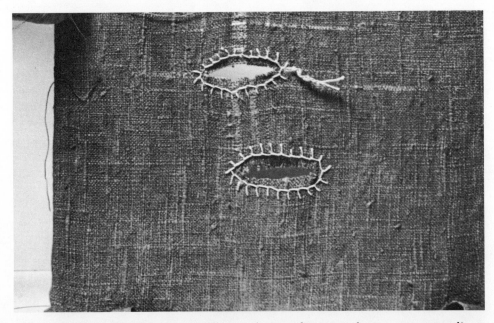

Henry Stahmer demonstrates a modern technique for using the reverse cut applique idea. Simply cut a shape in the fabric and outline with any kind of stitch (here he uses a blanket stitch) and place another fabric beneath it. This process could be repeated with more than two layers.

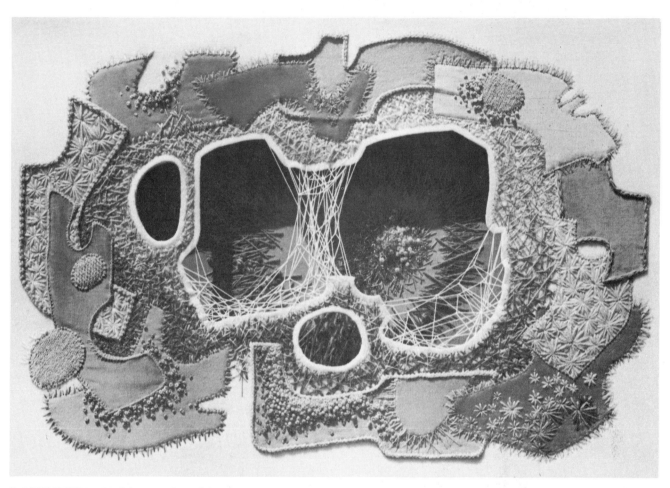

LORENTZEN. Wilcke Smith. 24″ high, 26″ wide. Made on heavy double-ply white coat wool on a 2″ deep redwood frame. The back surface of the frame is covered with a pale tan fine corduroy worked with appliques of peach velvet, clusters of copper and glass beads, and masses of fine, curled copper wire. The front plane of the frame is covered with a white coat wool that has been appliqued with a variety of warm greens in velvet and wool. The coat wool has been cut through to reveal the back panel; the apertures have been partially laced over with white yarn. COLLECTION: DR. & MRS. E. J. LORENTZEN, ALBUQUERQUE. PHOTO, BOB SMITH

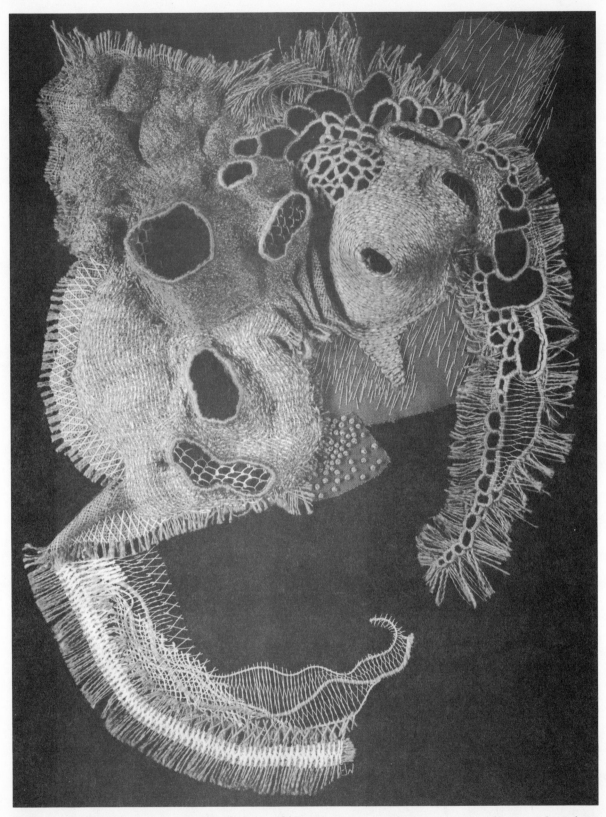

THE CACHE. Evelyn Svec Ward. 25″ high, 19¼″ wide. Direct applique, reverse applique, and stitchery are all combined in this rich use of fabrics, techniques, and design. Materials include burlap, cotton, Mexican maguey netting, threads of string, cotton jutes, and synthetics on wool backing. PHOTO, WILLIAM E. WARD

U.F.O. Evelyn Svec Ward. 44″ high, 16½″ wide. Stitchery and cut work using burlap, cotton floss, crochet cotton, and synthetic fabrics. Stitches are worked from a piece of burlap in the center formed into a three-dimensional shape.
PHOTO, WILLIAM E. WARD

94

C FOR 7 FRED. Marilyn Pappas. 38″ high, 28″ wide. Army shirt, yarns, ropes, buttons, trimmings on a heavy woven backing have the quality of a deep relief sculpture done with fabrics. The square and rectangle are ignored as the fabrics burst their bounds into space.

5   Mixed Media with Stitchery

There are critics who insist on relating stitchery only to a craft and define it, therefore, as "useful, decorative: meant to enhance the surfaces of clothing, purses, household accessories, such as tablecloths and linens." Embroidery falls under this definition, but there is a great difference between embroidery and stitchery as it is practiced today. People who are stitchers work with the elements of the fine artist and their results are exciting and expressive. An imaginary cultural lag appears to exist in the minds of critics who have not taken a long, hard, educated look at stitchery activity today.

Not only are painters and sculptors employing stitchery, but the stitcher, also a fine artist, is employing other media: paint, collage, metal sculpture, ceramics, found object art, etc., to the picture plane.

Display and promotion outlets for the serious stitcher are multipying. There is the excellent *Craft Horizons* Magazine published by the American Crafts Council. In the past ten years many states have formed Designer-Craftsmen Groups, which sponsor art shows. More and more art galleries are bringing in work that bridges both crafts and arts. Sales potential is still limited by the unsophisticated buyer, but textile arts departments of major museums are making purchases.

The following examples illustrate the direction stitchery is taking when it is combined with other art media. They also illustrate another approach to help broaden your own development of stitcheries and to emphasize the exploratory nature and aesthetics of this art. The works frequently use the principles of sculpture: they exist in space; often space becomes a part of the work; concepts of volume, light, line, shape, and motions are as important to stitchery composition as to other works of art.

Except for the addition of other media, the stitches used are the same as those developed in Chapter 2. Other essential ingredients are inspiration and imagination, which are as easy to develop as any other aspect of technique—so long as one has the interest. One can achieve the *joie de vivre* of Joan Miro, the hard-edged precision of Joseph Stella, or the inventiveness of Pablo Picasso. Only the medium—stitchery—is different.

Detail of above

Collage or paper collé can be combined with stitchery. Henry Stahmer glued shapes of different colored art tissues, Japanese rice papers, and sometimes magazine pages to his canvas. Suggesting a stitchery design, the materials at the same time add colors to the surface beneath the stitches.

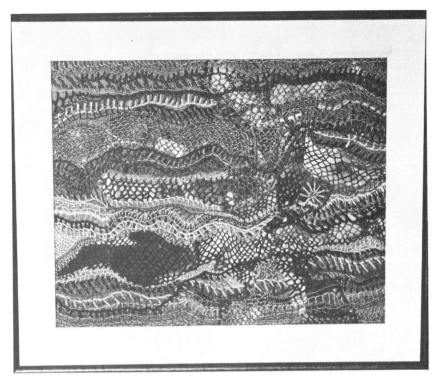

MOSS GARDEN. Henry Stahmer. 18″ high, 22″ wide. Stitchery with collage of paper shapes cut from a magazine and glued to linen fabric. The stitchery imposed on paper and backing.

For a combination of design techniques, one might bleach out the fabric as shown in Chapter 3. Place shapes of contrasting colored tissue on the base fabric. Proceed using yarns and stitches creatively. TECHNIQUE, HENRY STAHMER

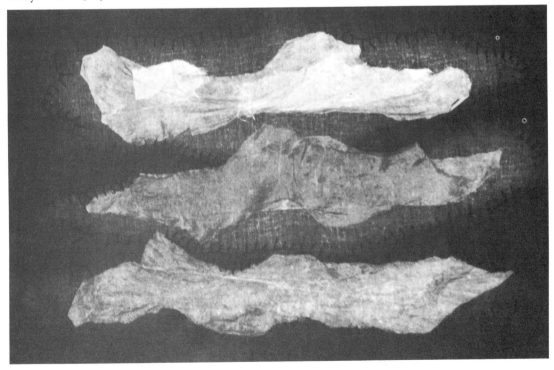

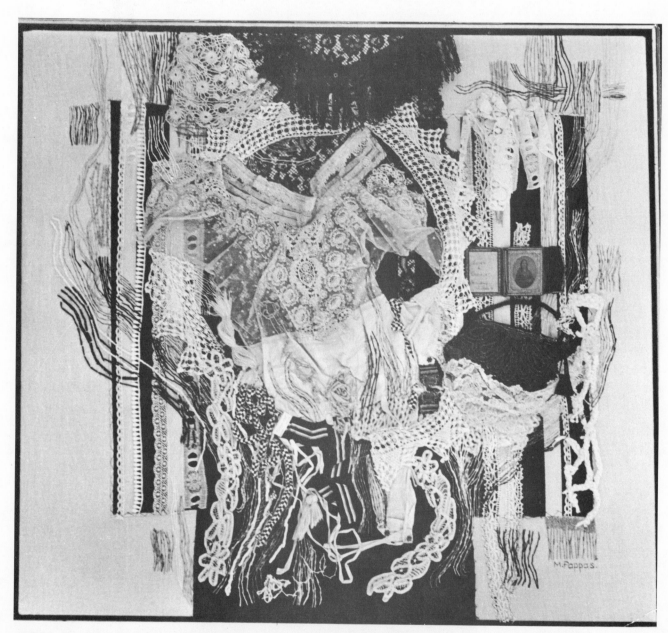

COLLAGE IN BLACK AND WHITE. Marilyn Pappas. 37″ high, 47″ wide. Antique clothing, assorted trimmings, yarns, threads, laces, frame, a purse, and other mementos. PHOTO, KLARA FARKAS

SUN BIRD. Lucille Brokaw. 60″ high, 45″ wide. Painted canvas background with stitchery shows how media may be combined successfully.

Space penetrates all these hangings and becomes a part of the composition.

WEAVING. Sherrill Kahn. 24″ high, 18″ wide. Stitchery and knotting used with hand-woven tapestry.

FISH TREE HOUSE. Nell Booker Sonnemann. 81″ high, 48″ wide. Free form hanging of batik fabric plus plain fabrics. Cotton, wool, padding, synthetic materials, hand and zig-zag machine sewing. COURTESY, ARTIST

PUTAO. Helen L. Breunig. 54″ high, 72″ wide. Red silk and wool tassel fringe, velvet, cotton, beads, silver, bangles using applique, stitchery, and hand tie. PHOTO, CALIFORNIA DESIGN X, PASADENA ART MUSEUM

STILL LIFE. Norma C. Minkowitz. 32″ high, 26″ wide. Black nylon twill is wrapped around a frame and glued. Then black nylon thread is strung crosswise and lengthwise, creating a surface to work upon. The design was created by detached blanket stitches, straight stitching, and back stitches, providing movement and variety in weight and space. COURTESY, ARTIST

102

A SHAGGY DOG STORY COMPLETE WITH COLLAR. Vesta Ward. Padded felt with surface stitching in fine yarns and rug yarns. Shaggy felt strips go beyond surface plane. Reds and oranges predominate, and a red doughnut turns freely within the canvas. COURTESY, ARTIST

BALLOONS. Charlotte Newfeld. 15" high, 12" wide. Ceramic shapes for dresses and arms add to the relief treatment of the padded balloons stuffed with cardboard from egg cartons and scrap fabrics attached with a satin stitch.

NIGHTMOON. Pat Tavenner. 14″ high, 16″ wide. Photos silk-screened on fabrics and then fabrics stitched on to backing by hand and machine. COURTESY, ARTIST

WEBBED FRAGMENT. Doris Hoover. Spidery feeling of yarns echo the patterns of nature's fernery. Varied yarns, copper wire, metal nuts in network over tacks on weathered wood. PHOTO, MARGARET VAILE

THE NATURE OF MATERIALS. Alma Lesch. Richly stitched soft hanging has a sculptural effect. Combined are stitchery with hooking and knotting and window shade pulls on linen and burlap. COLLECTION: MRS. DOROTHY COLLEY, ANCHORAGE, KENTUCKY

BUBBLE AND SQUEAK. Martha Underwood. 36″ high, 30″ wide. Combination of lace, weaving, and applique techniques. Some of the padded areas have "squeakies" in them that sound out when pushed.
COURTESY, ARTIST

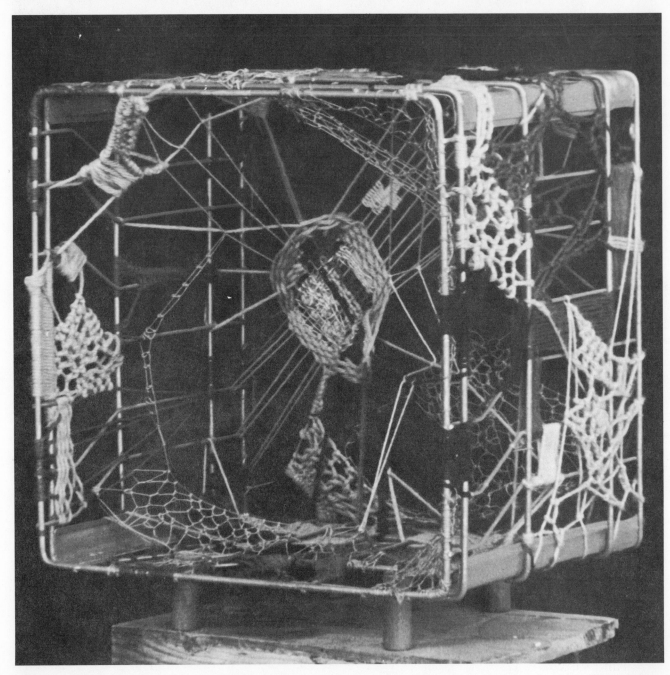

CRAZY SPIDER. Doris Hoover. Varied threads in hot colors worked over a square wire form from a milk crate from which the bottom was removed. PHOTO, MARGARET VAILE

6 Sculptural Stitchery

The creation of sculptural stitchery appears to be a recent invention. Much of it is meant to be as pure an art form as is a sculpture of wood, marble, or bronze. Sometimes the artist combines the sculptural medium successfully with a useful object such as a chair, footstool, or room divider, thus emphasizing the impossibility of drawing a distinction between craftsman and artist.

From the examples shown, it is apparent that stitchery is not limited to surface-decorating a solid piece of fabric. So long as there is some kind of base on which to hang the stitches and other materials, it is possible to create stitcheries that are open and three dimensional.

Much of the work depends on experimentation, on being able to visualize how an object will fit into the scheme of things. Doris Hoover's use of a metal milk container as her framework illustrates the trend toward found objects in this, as in many other, art forms.

With so much art dependent upon the machine age, it is conceivable that stitcheries could be formed over gears, over outmoded motors, using scores of items available at the hardware store. An entire stitchery could be worked through the holes of a sheet of screening bent to a sculptural form. It is possible that someone unwilling to part with a cherished child's buggy or bicycle will use it as a base for an expressive, creative stitchery. A wicker basket, chair, or desk item could be successfully converted into sculpture, using imagination, fabric, and yarn.

That is the message of this entire book: there is no one way to create art, no one best way to work with any of the materials. The examples offered are meant to stimulate you to be innovative. If this book has helped generate that stimulation, it has served its purpose. In addition, it has brought together, for the first time, examples of some of the most creative stitchers working today.

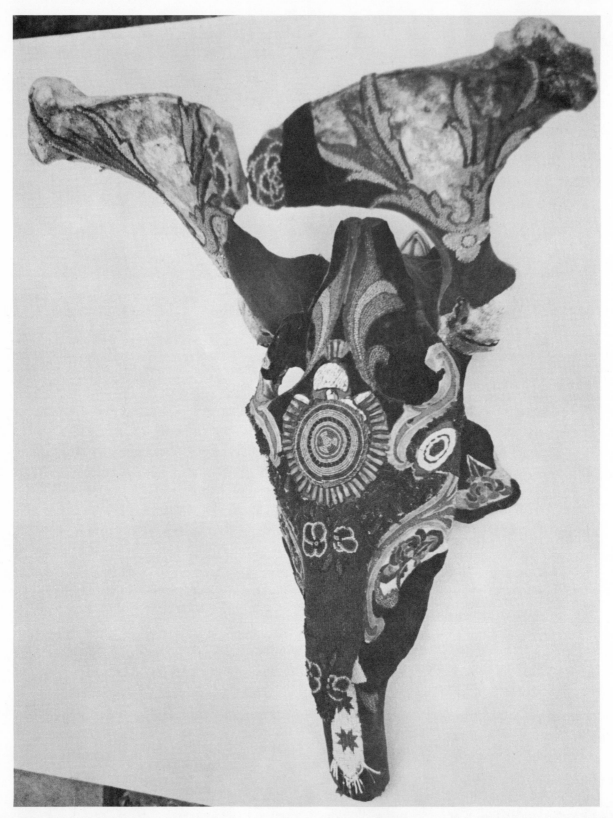

BEADED COW'S SKULL. Carol McPhee. Actual pelvic bones used for base. Covered with red and blue velvet, then glass beads, abalone shell, and silk stitchery. COURTESY, ARTIST

MUSHROOM. M. Sunnergren. 15″ high and 18″ wide. Woolen fabrics and yarns machine and hand stitched over a wood core. Top is stuffed with kapok. Bottom view below. COURTESY, ARTIST

MASK. Norma Minkowitz. 27″ high, 12″ wide. Three-dimensional mask using reverse applique technique. Four layers of fabric with black "applique on" areas. Stitched on chicken wire and bent to achieve a cylindrical effect. COURTESY, ARTIST

FROZEN STREAM. Jo Willrodt. 48″ high, 18″ wide. Shaped from aluminum screen with bound edges. Fabrics then overlaid, including cottons, fishnet, beads, a tree branch. Yarns of nylon, swiss-straw, wool, and cotton. PHOTO, MARGARET VAILE

THE EGG. Anna M. Sunnergren. 12″ high. Soft sculpture of burlap and white cotton cord, machine and hand stitched. A shape inside represents an egg yolk and moves around freely. COURTESY, ARTIST

FREE FORM SCULPTURE. Joyce Wexler. 22″ high, 14″ wide. Fur, fabric, and fruit pits on a wood base. The fur tail at the bottom is movable and may be changed as the viewer wishes. The core is a sofa pillow.

GUARDIAN ANGEL. Berni Gorski. Lace weaving and stitchery on metal armatures. The head is a metal cube shape, with a wire basket for the crown. Wings are carpet beaters; old lace is stretched over the beaters. Hair is made of tiny, jet-black beads. PHOTO, HENRY GORSKI

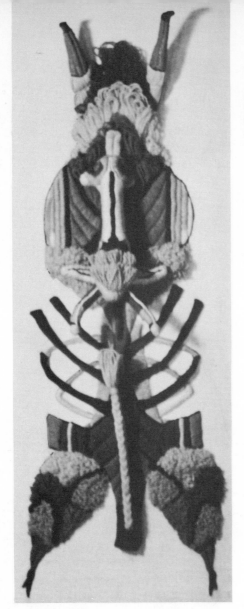

FLAYED BULL. Charlotte Newfeld. Applique, stitchery, and hooking over a frame of wire and masonite, cut to shapes.

CUBE. Ronald M. Rolfe. 12″ square. Abstract shapes suggest the map of the world. Felt and paisley prints with machine and hand stitchery. Made of white pine covered first with a white felt liner, then with colored felt. Top fabrics should be cut to cube shape, then machine and hand stitched before attaching them to cube. COLLECTION: DR. & MRS. MEL MEILACH, CHICAGO

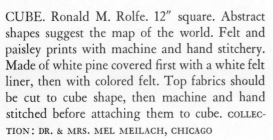

THE SUN IS MY UNDOING. Doris Hoover. 24″ high, 36″ wide, 8″ deep. Wire frame with fabric, mesh hose, fish netting stretched over it; stitches worked in various threads. Some fabric doubled and machine stitched for body. PHOTO, MARGARET VAILE

LAMPSHADE FOR TAMIS. Doris
Hoover. 20″ high, 14″ diameter. Nylon
net and stitchery of wool, cotton, rayon,
silk, and swiss-straw over a wire frame.
PHOTO, MARGARET VAILE

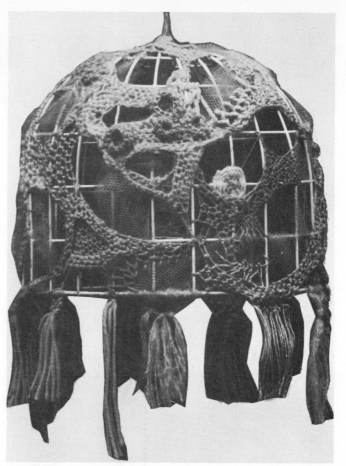

CHAIR WITH BIRDS. Berni Gorski. 28″ high,
17″ wide. Lace weaving with black yarns; birds
are red, yellow, and blue. Chair is usable and has
a black modacrylic seat. PHOTO, HENRY GORSKI

TWO-FOLD LACERY SCREEN. Evelyn Svec Ward. 61″ high, 36″ wide. Ropes, yarns, and strings of many fabrics are combined in this "lacery" created within a wooden frame using all kinds of stitching and knotting techniques, plus knitted pieces stretched, pulled, and worked in. PHOTO, WILLIAM E. WARD

Index